THE OBLIGATION TO REMEMBER

THE AMERICAN GATHERING OF JEWISH HOLOCAUST SURVIVORS
WASHINGTON, D.C.
APRIL 11-14, 1983

AN ANTHOLOGY BY THE STAFF OF

The Washington Post

I t is now 38 years since the defeat of Hitler's empire and the Allied armies' relief of the death camps. Anyone who survived those camps is now well into middle age; most are elderly. That is the reason for the American Gathering of Jewish Holocaust Survivors. It is preparation for a time when there will no longer be living witnesses to those events.

Some of those who died in the camps were Gypsies, and some were intellectuals. Some were Christians whose consciences made them disruptive influences in Hitler's New Order. But a very great majority of them were, of course, Jews, sent there in the empire's attempt to destroy a faith together with all who followed it and their families. In Europe, that attempt nearly succeeded. The Holocaust will necessarily have a special meaning for Jews, but it would be deeply wrong to let the memory of the death camps be consigned to an exclusively Jewish heritage. The message of the Holocaust deserves the most careful consideration of everyone of any religion or none at all.

Even in 1945, in the heat of war, the significance of the Holocaust transcended national politics. It was correctly taken as evidence of the presence of a militant and purposeful evil, in the sense in which the moralists and theologians have always used the word. There had been optimistic times in the 18th and 19th centuries when enlightened people often thought of evil as a condition that rising standards of living and improved education would eventually cure. That brave thought collapsed in the first half of the present century. The death camps were the creation of people who were highly endowed, by the world's standards, with both material wealth and an elevated culture. The 1930s and the 1940s brought the demonstration that the heart of darkness does not lie in the upper reaches of some exotic or primitive place, but much closer to home, in the most "advanced" of societies. The death camps stand in our history as profound warning against certain dangerously easy assumptions about human nature. The camps constitute a commentary not simply on Nazi Germany, but on habits of mind and spirit that can be found elsewhere as well.

It is more pleasant not to think about these things, and to keep the conversation to those moments in history that show the human race at its best. But at the other extreme are those stark camps still within the memory of people here in this city, conveying their own terrible instruction. That is the point of the gathering here. There is a moral obligation to remember — always.

Editorial, The Washington Post
April 11, 1983

CONTENTS

" *Never say that you are going your last way.*
Though lead-filled skies above blot out the blue of day.
The hour for which we long will certainly appear.
The earth shall thunder 'neath our tread that we are here! **"**

From *Mir Zeyhen Do* "We Are Here,"
The Song of the Warsaw Ghetto Resisters.

A FIVE-FAMILY ANTHOLOGY: HORRORS OF THE HOLOCAUST

BY BLAINE HARDEN

The SS, with their whips and dogs and jackboots, have marched for 38 years through the death-camp nightmares of Mike Jacobs.

Now 57 and the owner of a scrap-metal business in Dallas, Jacobs was 16 years old in Ostroweic, Poland, when he was forced to carry babies to the roof of a building where German soldiers threw them to the sidewalk for sport. He was 18 when a guard at Birkenau sliced open his face with a whip, and, fearing the gas chambers that awaited those who appeared weak, he fashioned six aluminum clamps to hold his face together. He was 19½ years old, a 70-pound man-child whose parents and five brothers and sisters were all killed, when American soldiers liberated him near Mauthausen, Austria, on May 5, 1945.

In his dreams, the SS soldiers try again and again to kill him.

"They take me outside, whipping and kicking me all over," says Jacobs. "They beat me and torture me, but I always come out the winner and never let them kill me. I stand up to them. I wake up in a sweat with a smile on my face. I won."

Jacobs is one of the thousands of European-born American Jews who won, who survived the Holocaust and who came to Washington to commemorate their victory over Adolf Hitler's attempt to annihilate what he called "the Jewish race in Europe."

By normal standards, they are strangers to each other. Their homes are scattered across the United States and Canada. They are middle-aged and elderly Jewish immigrants from Germany, Poland, Austria, Czechoslovakia, Hungary, Romania, Bulgaria, Denmark, Latvia, Lithuania and other war-scarred European countries. They are of different classes and many have fallen away from the Jewish religion.

But as they come to record their names and Holocaust histories in a computer registry and attempt to find lost relatives and friends, they bring memories that bind them in a fraternity of witnesses.

"Those who have not lived through the experience will never know; those who have will never tell; not really, not completely," writes Elie Wiesel, a survivor, theologian and keynote speaker for the gathering. "The survivor knows. He and no one else."

By their numbers and the very fact that they are alive while the Third Reich is dead, they have come to Washington in shared triumph.

"It is 40 years later, Hitler is dead and we are here," says Herman Taube, a survivor, poet and local organizer of the gathering.

The writer Cynthia Ozick, in a recent short story, wrote that Holocaust survivors have three separate lives: "the life before, the life during, the life after." For decades in the United States, survivors have themselves censored the "during" from their own lives. It was too gruesome for nonsurvivors to hear or believe, too painful for many survivors to share with their own children.

The gathering of Jewish Holocaust survivors was planned, in part, for survivors to exorcise the "curing," to share their long-private torment and draw comfort from the select and dwindling few whose strength and luck permitted them to live while millions around them were killed.

"Even to find someone who sat on the same bench in a concentration camp means something," says Taube.

Most of the survivors who have come here this week, organizers say, are strong people, such as Jacobs, the Dallas scrap dealer. Like Jacobs, they are now capable of discussing the atrocities that were visited upon them and their families.

An estimated 100,000 to 200,000 survivors of the Holocaust came to the United States after World War II. Of the 45,000 who are known to be still alive, Holocaust scholars say there are thousands who still cannot discuss what happened to them, who have burdened their children with guilt, who are upset that other survivors would gather to commemorate the unspeakable.

In the Washington area, for example, there is a Polish-born survivor who is outraged that Jews would commemorate their own destruction. For years, this man, who escaped a death camp in Poland shortly before his parents were killed, ordered his children not to laugh or sing in his Bethesda home. He will not attend.

In Silver Spring there is another Polish American who will not attend. At Auschwitz, at the train ramp where SS doctors separated those who would live from those who would die, this man's wife refused to give up her baby. She and the baby were sent to the right, to the gas chambers. He was sent to the left, to a work camp. He often wakes up in the night screaming his wife's name.

In a Maryland mental hospital, there is a Latvian survivor of the Kaiserwald and Stutthof camps. He was beaten by the SS and his family was murdered. He came to Washington in the late '40s, established a successful roofing business and was active in Washington-area survivor organizations. But he often told friends he "didn't deserve" to be happy. He divorced two wives, gave up his business and committed himself to the hospital.

For five of the families who will be at the gathering, however, there has been a different experience. These survivors have made successful lives for themselves in the United States. They all say they are happy. They have lived for years with horrible nightmares, though for some the nightmares have stopped.

Few of them can yet muster the strength to tell their children an unabridged version of the atrocities they saw. They talk most easily to fellow survivors. They are attempting, sometimes without much success, to remember the Holocaust and at the same time to get on with their lives.

These survivors, some of whom are speaking for the first time, say they are telling their

> **"We knew there was danger coming in. I was maybe 20, but what could I do? Why didn't I flee? In the Jewish tradition the family is always knit very close. I had a chance to escape. How could I in my mind save myself and leave my father and mother helpless? Of course, it didn't do them any good that I stayed."**

Edward Golfer, 62,
Silver Spring carryout owner.
Born in Kaunas, Lithuania.
Imprisoned at Stutthof
and Dachau.

stories because they want no one to deny or forget what happened to them.

THE TAUBES

In 1947, the year Herman and Susan Taube arrived in Baltimore, they were invited to speak about the Holocaust at a Hanukkah party.

"I started talking," remembers Taube, "and shared with them our life and this woman said to me, 'Come on, we can live without hearing that. More music. Start the music.' The orchestra played and they began to dance. My wife went home in tears."

Taube was not discouraged. He has gone on speaking, writing [five novels, three books of poetry] and organizing survivors ever since. During the war, he served as a medic in the Polish army and, after liberation, treated death-camp survivors. He met and fell in love with his wife, a survivor of many camps, when she was emaciated and ill. Now an official with the United Jewish Appeal of Greater Washington, Taube, 65, says his obsession with the Holocaust is "a religious calling."

Susan (Strauss) Taube, 57, did not speak at that Hanukkah party back in Baltimore. Until last week, she has said very little about the Holocaust. She says her husband sometimes talks too much. "When I talk," she says, "I see pictures."

When she was seven years old in Vacha, Germany, the Nazi brown shirts began to break windows of Jewish homes. "I was sleeping with my little sister and they throw stones through the windows and we slept in glass. All night long we slept in glass."

As a German Jew, Susan's "pictures" of the Holocaust span from 1933 when the Nazis forced a boycott of her father's clothing store until 1945 when the Russians liberated her in a barn in Poland. Her father escaped to America in 1938 but could not get his wife or two daughters out. Her mother and sister were killed in Polish death camps. When the Russians liberated the barn, they raped all those who were strong enough to run outside. Susan, 19 years old, a veteran of 12 years of violence, was too weak to run. She was not raped.

The Taubes moved to Baltimore after the war because Susan's father was there. They moved in with him. She does not know if her father, now dead, felt guilty that he escaped while his family suffered. "I don't know what he felt," says Susan, "I never talked to him; he never asked."

The Taubes, who now live in Aspen Hill, have five children and seven grandchildren. Their closest friends over the years have been survivors.

"We never feel so much at home as when we are with survivors," says Herman, who helped start survivors' clubs in Baltimore and Washington. "We sit for five minutes and we start talking about the camps."

THE GODINS

Jack Godin, 61, a Silver Spring glazier whose parents were killed by Nazis in Poland, does not speak of the Holocaust. His wife, Nesse, 55, does all the talking.

"I talk and he keeps quiet. It hurts him too much," says Godin, who speaks to church groups, schools, anyone who asks for her story. Sitting at her dining room table recently, interrupting her Passover cooking, Nesse Godin talked.

She was 13 years old, "a little shnook," when the Germans in 1941 occupied her hometown of Siauliai, Lithuania. They herded 1,000 Jewish men outside town to dig trenches in the forest called Bubiai. "They were made to get undressed naked and shot," said Godin. In the same way, a short time later, 3,500 Jews, including orphans and the elderly, were taken outside Siauliai and shot.

"We still did not face realities," Godin said. "Would you believe I would stand up now and go in my kitchen and come with a gun and kill you? Would you believe me that? In modern times, people should kill people for no reason whatsoever?"

Nazis forced all the Jews older than 15 into a camp, a ghetto, on the outskirts of Siauliai. Godin's mother bribed a local woman to smuggle her underage daughter into the camp. Thus began four years in concentration and death camps.

Her father was taken to Auschwitz and gassed in 1943. Godin was taken the next year in a cattle car to Poland, separated from her mother and forced to dig tank-trap trenches. At Stutthof camp, she sorted shoes of the dead and stuffed mattresses with human hair. She was protected by an older woman, a stranger who at night hid Godin's bread between her breasts to keep it from thieves. On a "death march" to the Baltic Sea, Godin was hit in the face with the butt of a rifle. She remains scarred with what she calls a "beauty mark."

"I have a sense of humor, see. I never cry, but I have a sense of humor."

After liberation, she met Jack Godin in a displaced persons camp ("a nice young man hanging around with us with nobody in the world"). They were married immediately and came to Washington in 1950. Jack got a job as a glazier; Nesse, for 23 years, was a dressmaker. They have three children and Nesse speaks proudly of "my happy life in the beautiful United States." Her mother and her two brothers also survived.

"I am a fortunate woman," said Godin. "My mother lived, survived the Holocaust, came to this country, saw me get married, saw me have children. She got sick and she died at the age of 69. She lived a normal cycle. She is buried on Adelphi Road in a cemetery. She has a nice beautiful stone there. I can come, I can say, 'My dear mother, God took you, you died, nobody killed you.'

"For my father, nothing. For my grandparents, for my aunts, my uncles, my husband's family . . . nothing."

THE MASTERS

Peter Arany (he later took the name Masters) escaped from Vienna and Alice Eberstarkova escaped from her Czechoslovakian village before the killing began.

The Nazis took control of Vienna in March 1938, when Peter was 15 years old. The son of a jeweler, he was a cosmopolitan young man who loved Verdi and van Gogh and kept a diary. In it, he recorded what he saw as Nazi crimes. Well-dressed Jews were ordered to scrub streets on their hands and knees. Elderly Jews who lined up for soup were forced to do calisthenics. A newspaper ran a photo of a "mixed-race" baby with the caption: "Note particularly the evil look in the eyes of the baby."

"You see how mild it sounds compared to subsequent atrocities, but at the time it was absolutely unbelievable," says Masters, 61. "We were too cultured and far too civilized . . ."

In the summer of 1939, when hundreds of Viennese Jewish intellectuals committed suicide, Masters, along with his mother and sister, obtained passage on a train out of Austria.

(Top) Deportation of Jews from Baden-Baden to concentration camps after the destruction of Jewish-owned stores, businesses and synagogues on Kristallnacht (November 9, 1938). The sign on the Star of David says, "God will not forsake us."
(Left) Herman and Susan Taube in 1945. He nursed his wife back to health after both survived concentration camps.
(Above) The Dutch version of the Star of David that the Nazis required Jews to wear throughout Europe.

In London, after hearing that his grandfather had been killed at Auschwitz, Masters joined a unit of British commandos. He fought in the invasion of Normandy and across France to the Rhine. At his enlistment, he said: "Sir, they killed my grandfather. I believe part of the action is mine."

Alice Eberstarkova and her two sisters are the only Jewish survivors of the Tatra Mountain village of Trstena. Her parents, after spending most of their savings on three passports, loaded them on a train that left Bratislava in July 1939. Her mother, sobbing with indecision, took Alice's 10-year-old sister off the train twice. When the train finally pulled away, she lifted the little girl aboard. Alice's parents and grandparents were taken in 1942 to Auschwitz and killed.

"There is never a day when I don't think about it," says Alice Masters, 57, who does not talk to friends about the Holocaust. "I never take a shower without thinking about the showers, the gas. I never go to the kitchen to peel a potato, without saying to myself, 'What those people would have given to eat these peels.'"

The Masters, who came to Washington in 1948, live in Bethesda. He is a graphic designer; she recently retired from the International Monetary Fund. They have three children. Their daughter Kim, when she was 14, wrote a poem about the Nazis and grandparents she could never know. It concluded: "Creators of hell on earth. I curse you with all my being for this robbery."

THE DIAMENTS

Stefan and Henrietta Diament, who live now in Memphis where they own the Diamond Printing Company, were engaged to be married in 1939 when the German army occupied Lodz, Poland.

Thinking that Warsaw would be safer, Henrietta Leszczynski, the daughter of a wealthy textile manufactuer, and her fiancé, a skilled printer, drove a truck north to the Polish capital. They were married, and, within weeks, were confined inside the Warsaw ghetto. There, they began six years of "organizing" — the survivors' term for trading, lying and stealing to stay alive.

For four years they remained in the ghetto, moving constantly, sometimes crawling out windows in the night, as 400,000 other Jews were sent away, most of them to the gas chambers of Treblinka. After the Jewish uprising of April 1943, Nazis set the ghetto afire. "We were fortunate to be deported to the camps instead of being shot there," says Henrietta.

At Maidanek concentration camp, they were separated. Stefan was sent to work in aircraft plants in Poland and Germany. "I found out printer they don't need, so I told them I was mechanic," says Stefan. He ate relatively well and worked inside. Working conditions were tense. "When a man drilled a hole in a wrong place, they hanged him right there in the factory . . . If someone ran away, they lined us all up in a circle and shoot every 10th person."

Henrietta was sent to farming camps near Radom and in 1944, en route to Auschwitz, she tried to escape by jumping off a train. "I was lucky they didn't shoot me. They just whip me," she says. "They shot others who tried."

Their luck held till liberation. They were reunited in Belgium. Stefan showed up at a prearranged meeting place where Henrietta had waited for three weeks. "I was the one who opened the door," says Henrietta, "and we lived happily since, which is the truth."

The Diaments have two sons, one a doctor, the other an engineer who recently has come to work in the family printing business in Memphis. Neither Stefan nor Henrietta talks to their sons about the Holocaust.

"We never really sat down and told them because there is no way to explain this," says Henrietta. "Whatever they asked, they got straight answers. They were afraid to ask too much. Our sons are achievers.

"People are surprised how healthy mentally we are. We have a straight and sensible attitude toward life. We nurture our families. They are very precious to us. I realized that I don't have to be afraid that anyone will take my sons away from me."

MIKE JACOBS

Mike Jacobs was an "organizer" from the time he was 12 years old in the ghetto in Ostrowiec. "I didn't look Jewish," he says, so he could move in and out of the ghetto, trading pants and shirts made by his three brothers — all tailors — for eggs and bread.

When the Nazis made a "selection" he said he had a "feeling" he should not go to the "big square" with his family. He sneaked off to a side street. His family was sent to Treblinka and the gas chambers.

While he was "organizing" to stay alive, Jacobs said he had no idea there were gas chambers at Treblinka or anywhere else. He didn't find out until, at age 18, he arrived at Auschwitz in 1944.

"It was a very nice day when we stepped down off the train," remembers Jacobs. "An orchestra [of Jewish musicians] was playing. I said to my friend, 'It looks like a paradise and it is so clean . . .' I saw the four chimneys [of the crematoria]. I thought they were baking a lot of bread for all the workers. I decided that when they asked my occupation, I would say baker. But they never asked me.

"I came closer to the chimneys. I said to my friend, 'You know what? That aroma is not bread. It is a different smell.' It smelled like hides. They are killing so many horses; they are burning hides."

At Birkenau, the camp that adjoined Auschwitz, Jacobs found out what they were burning. Within weeks, he was trading with Poles who lived nearby, exchanging gold teeth, jewels and money — taken from the dead — for bread.

When he was liberated, Jacobs made his way west and went to work in an American army kitchen in Germany. "Where the food was," he says. He came to Dallas in 1951, sponsored by the Jewish Welfare Federation.

Teaching physical fitness in a Jewish community center, he met his wife, a native Texan. They have four children: a married daughter and three sons — a lawyer, a college student and one who works with his father at the Jacobs Iron and Metal Company.

"At the moment my children could understand," Jacobs says, "I was explaining what I come from, what I came through, what I am.

"I am not a bitter person. I do not hate. I am normal. I am healthy and I am happy . . . I am the lucky one. I can be here and tell the world that six million died because they were Jews."

A Nazi stationed outside a Jewish store on Boycott Day in 1933. The sign reads: "Germans! Defend yourselves! Don't buy from Jews!"

THE MAN WHO KNEW THE NAZI SECRET

BY CHARLES FENYVESI

In 1942 a German industrialist risked his life by revealing the secret of Hitler's order to exterminate European Jewry.

Only one person is still alive who knows this man's identity. He is Gerhart Riegner. He is now a portly, pink-cheeked gentleman of 71. Dressed in a three-piece suit, of a heavy woolen cloth of midnight blue, he looks like the mayor of a Swiss town: stolid, somber and exceedingly respectable.

During the war, Riegner was — and is still — the representative in neutral Geneva of the World Jewish Congress. Then he was a brilliant young legal counsel; now his title is secretary general. Then he was a refugee from Germany, one of the few the Swiss agreed to admit. He still travels with the *laissez-passer* of a stateless refugee; after close to 50 years of residence, he hasn't been able to bring himself to apply for Swiss citizenship and passport.

"It took two days to persuade myself that the industrialist was telling the truth," Riegner now says, "and finally I came to the conclusion that it was possible and probable." Riegner then went to the American and British diplomatic representatives and asked them to transmit the information to their governments and to key Jewish leaders.

That now-famous telegram — sent Aug. 8, 1942 — and others that followed were curtly dismissed in the State Department and Whitehall as "the opinion of one Jew in Geneva."

The State Department advised the U.S. legation in Switzerland that Riegner's charges were "unsubstantiated" and waited for 20 days to send a copy to Rabbi Stephen Wise, the key American Jewish leader of the time, to whom Riegner had originally addressed his cable. "[Undersecretary of State] Sumner Welles told Wise not to publish it," Riegner says. "In wartime it was an order."

For several months, no Allied or neutral official believed the industrialist, who heard about the plan during his many visits to Hitler's headquarters. He had free access to top Nazis because his factories, with their 30,000 skilled workers, were pressed into the service of the German war machine. The industrialist's fervent hope was that once the world learned of the death camps, it would do something to stop them.

"Nobody really believed it," Riegner says. "Not even Jews who knew it. For instance, at the height of the extermination policy, I counted four million Jews as dead. My own office in New York — where I sent all my reports and which was directed by a great Jewish leader — published the figure of only 1.5 million."

The recent controversy over the Holocaust Inquiry Commission led by former Supreme Court Justice Arthur J. Goldberg deals in large part with what American Jewish organizations did or did not do in response to Riegner's cable. Riegner says he welcomes an impartial inquiry by independent scholars. But, he charges, the commission as it is now constituted is "ideologically fueled by people determined to rewrite history." The people Riegner criticizes are associates of Israeli Prime Minister Menachem Begin, "who want to indict the Zionist establishment" of neglecting rescue work.

Riegner tells how another American Jewish leader sent him a list of 30,000 addresses of Jews in Poland and asked the Geneva office to send food packages to those addresses. "That was in 1943 or '44," Riegner says. "What madness! They saw all my reports and knew that none of those addresses were valid. Those people were . . ."

Riegner doesn't complete the sentence. He stares into space, purses his lips and declares slowly, flatly, impassively: "They knew it but they didn't believe it."

Riegner, however, was convinced. At 30, he was "an unexcitable, serious young man," he recalls, "always a well-balanced type." Having studied law in Germany and then in France, he intended to become a professor of jurisprudence. He saw himself as following in the footsteps of his father, once Germany's minister of justice, and a person drawn to the philosophy of law. "I come from a typically German-Jewish bourgeois family very deeply embedded in German culture, a humanistic tradition, interested in philosophy, history, art," Riegner says. "But also roots in Jewishness."

From the time Riegner saw Nazis beating up Jews and other political enemies on the streets and in the universities, he was a stiff pessimist in the face of what he calls "the Jewish optimism of the centuries — a kind of wishful thinking, really."

Unlike many other Jews, who dismissed Nazism as an episode and predicted that Hitler would soon run out of steam, Riegner argued that Jews should leave Germany while they still could — he left in May 1933, four months after Hitler became chancellor. He read *Mein Kampf* and listened to Nazi slogans and songs. "From my first encounter with Nazi terror, I took the Nazis seriously," he says. "Hitler made many speeches in which he threatened to destroy the totality of Jews.

"Why people didn't believe is a question I have always struggled with. It was so terrible that the human mind refused to accept it. An encounter with absolute evil is something very few people are prepared to accept. It is a paradox: The most positive experience is that people can't accept evil. That means that man is basically good."

At the time Riegner had no doubt: The industrialist was telling the truth, and all other evidence supported the report.

Headquartered in Geneva, only a few miles from Germany and France, Riegner collected information, all of which confirmed the industrialist's report. The list of witnesses grew every week. A Jew who survived two massacres (36,000 dead) in the ghetto of Riga and reached Switzerland; a Swiss employe in the consulate in Prague briefed by Czech Jews on deportations; a Polish Jew who was smuggled out of Russia by a disaffected German officer warning him about the extermination camps he had seen; messages, smuggled out by French railway workers, of mass roundups of West European Jews for transportation to concentration camps in the east.

There was even testimony from a Danish Jew close to Field Marshal Hermann Goering — "Goering had such strange associations," Riegner explains, "and we asked ourselves how reliable he was" — who somehow smuggled to Geneva a sheaf of the railroad schedules for Jewish transports. In a supreme example of bureaucratic punctiliousness, the German railways billed the Berlin Jewish community for the cost of the deportations.

Riegner kept filing the reports, kept asking for action. "We never did enough," he says. "Sure, we could have done more. All of us. In 1944 Wise finally got the American government to agree to a free port admitting 1,000 Yugoslav Jews. It was a procedure to postpone immigration problems. It could have been done with thousands of others. Also, we could have put stronger pressures on the neutrals — Sweden, Turkey — to accept more refugees. We could have brought more people to England, to North Africa.

"Hitler could have been stopped several times, but once he started rolling, only thousands, maybe tens of thousands of Jews could have been saved. Not millions."

The industrialist, ostensibly in Geneva on business, met Riegner three times, each time warning of the rising number of Jews being killed. He passed on details such as the kind of chemicals used in the gas chambers.

The industrialist was frustrated that nothing was happening, Riegner says. "In December 1942, finally, there was a condemnation of the massacres of Jews [from] London, Washington and Moscow. The British Parliament rose in two minutes of silence. But they wouldn't act."

Riegner says he does not know why the industrialist wanted to remain unknown. Fear of revenge against his family might have been a reason, Riegner says. He adds that it is possible that the industrialist never told his family about his role. "I wrote to his wife after his death," Riegner says, "and I alluded to his service. I think his wife might have known. Perhaps. But not his children. I don't know. For me, what mattered was that he was a democrat, deeply anti-Nazi — a man of great moral standards who wanted to relieve his conscience."

On one occasion, Riegner concedes, he was forced to reveal the industrialist's name. When he made "a desperate attempt" in the fall of 1942 to convince the Americans of the truth of the death camps, Riegner wrote down the industrialist's name, put it in a sealed envelope and handed it over to the head of the American legation in Bern. This was a few days after the industrialist had warned Riegner that he now had definite information on Hitler's direct order to exterminate all Jews. Riegner put all the evidence together in a document of 25 pages, to be transmitted to Washington.

But the envelope has disappeared, Riegner says, and an inkling of a sly grin spreads across his impassive face. The sealed envelope is not in the American archives, Riegner says, the U.S. diplomat is dead and no researcher has come up with the industrialist's name.

"I gave my word not to give out his name," Riegner now says. "I am bound to my word. He never asked for anything else. Many people have approached me to give out his name, but I did not break my word. I never will."

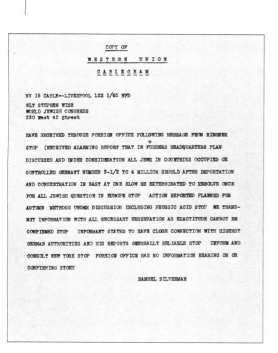

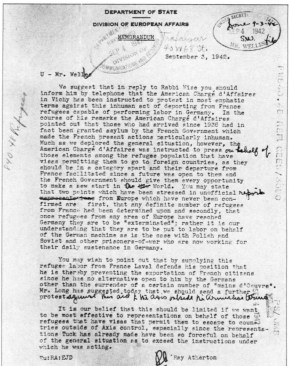

(Top) Gerhart Riegner in a 1983 photo. (Bottom, left to right) After Riegner sent his telegram to Samuel Silverman, a member of Parliament, Silverman sent a message to Rabbi Stephen Wise in New York. Wise then wrote to Undersecretary of State Sumner Welles. The European Affairs division of the State Department immediately drafted a proposed reply for Welles.

GIVING THANKS, HONORING THE DEAD

BY CARYLE MURPHY

"When the Nazis came in, right away it was bad. They were shooting from buses into crowds, at people on bread lines. They took out certain people for torture . . . German soldiers searched and took everything away. We remained without a penny to live from. Everything pointed to the bad times we were facing. Then they started to build a wall separating the Jews, starving the people. There was such sickness. People had no choice. We were ready to go to the death camps for a piece of bread."

Samuel Goldstein, 69, of Brooklyn. Born in Kozienice, Poland.

The formal opening of the American Gathering of Jewish Holocaust Survivors was held the evening of April 11, 1983 at the Capital Centre in Landover, Maryland.

Thousands of survivors of the Holocaust gathered last night to honor the dead, give thanks to America and applaud President Reagan when he pledged that "the security of your safe havens, here and in Israel, will never be compromised."

During a somber and emotional evening, the cavernous Capital Centre, usually the scene of sports and entertainment spectaculars, became more like a house of worship as six candles — symbolizing the six million Jews killed as part of Adolf Hitler's "Final Solution" — shone in the dark hall, and the audience, many of them weeping, chanted the Kaddish, the traditional Jewish prayer for the dead.

More than 15,000 people filled the arena in an unprecedented commemoration in this country of the Holocaust and its victims. The occasion was the opening assembly of the American Gathering of Jewish Holocaust Survivors, a four-day observance that brought to Washington more than 10,000 Holocaust survivors, the largest gathering of its kind ever held.

Many of the well-dressed, middle-aged people in the audience had come from a day of emotional reunions with old friends during the gathering's events at the Washington Convention Center when Reagan, accompanied by First Lady Nancy Reagan, made a brief address to open the evening.

Reagan's speech was punctuated throughout by applause from his listeners who filled the Landover arena almost to capacity. The other remark that brought heavy applause from the audience was Reagan's indirect challenge to the Soviet Union in mentioning Swedish diplomat Raoul Wallenberg, who saved many Jews during the war and is believed by many to be alive somewhere in a Soviet prison.

"I would affirm as President of the United States and if you would permit me, in the names of the survivors, that if those who took him from Budapest would win our trust, let them start by giving us an accounting of Raoul Wallenberg."

Reagan was presented with a scroll signed by more than 15,000 survivors thanking the U.S. armed forces who fought the Nazis and liberated thousands of Jews from Hitler's death camps. He and his wife then departed to the strains of "Exodus" played by the U.S. Navy Band.

Those thanks were also expressed by Benjamin Meed, the principal organizer of the gathering. "We have assembled here in our nation's capital — the world's greatest democracy — to give thanks to those hundreds of thousands who gave their lives to crush Hitler's Germany. We came to pay tribute to them and to thank you, America."

One of the themes of the gathering, besides the commemoration of the American government's efforts on behalf of Jews during and after World War II, is that mankind must be on constant guard to prevent another Holocaust.

Meed, a former resident of the Warsaw ghetto where a brave but futile uprising against Nazi occupiers took place 40 years ago April 19th, said the purpose of the gathering was to "keep the memory alive — and to warn the world again and again: Don't let this happen again."

Elie Wiesel, the Jewish writer, also spoke of the need to guard against conditions that would lead to persecutions. "We don't want pity; rather we want understanding, awareness. We want people to know that since this happened once, it must not happen again to anyone . . . We don't forget that once the killers began killing Jews, they began killing others."

Early in his speech Wiesel made an appeal to the friends of Israel to support that country and, in what many took to be a pointed reference to the recent pressures from Washington on Israel, he said that the tiny country was unique because it was "threatened militarily by its enemies and politically by its friends."

Although the organizers have downplayed the political aspects of the gathering, Meed also stated that one of the purposes of the assembly was also "to express our close ties to the State of Israel."

Reagan told the survivors that "as a man whose heart is with you — and as President of a people you are now so much a part of — I promise you that the security of your safe havens, here and in Israel, will never be compromised.

"Our most sacred task now is insuring that the memory of this greatest of human tragedies, the Holocaust, never fades . . ."

The observance, the president said, was also a means of recognizing those — some of them called "Righteous Gentiles" — whose moral fiber held firm during the days of the Holocaust as they sheltered and saved Jews.

Their moral character and consciousness must be fostered, he said, and Americans must recognize that for freedom to endure, it must be made innate so that "when confronted with fundamental choices we will do what is right, because that is our way."

Earlier, when participants in the observance arrived at the Washington Convention Center for registration, many of them, like Jando Weis, a carpenter from Cherry Hill, New Jersey, began searching for some scrap of information about relatives who were killed.

"I cannot give it up, " said Weis, 61. "This is the last hurrah. I'm not young any more."

Esther Milich Kozminski at the gathering, in search of her sister.

The text of American Gathering President Benjamin Meed's address to the opening ceremony of the American Gathering of Jewish Holocaust Survivors at the Capital Centre, Landover, Md., April 11, 1983.

My dear friends, my fellow survivors and distinguished guests:
Between the Warsaw Ghetto and Washington, between Auschwitz and America seems an incredible distance — a distance that goes beyond miles, beyond years — a distance between worlds, perhaps between universes.

It has been 40 years since I stood outside the walls of the burning Warsaw Ghetto and watched building after building engulfed by the flames and heard through the dense smoke the shooting and the screams of those trapped inside.

Forty years since I stood among the Poles posing as an Aryan and saw those around me indifferent to destruction of Jewish Warsaw.

Forty years, yet I can still smell the smoke in my nostrils, feel the heat upon my face. I remember it as only yesterday.

My friends, it seems a dream.

That we, the same people who were a part of the pulsating life of prewar Jewish Europe, the same people who struggled in the ghettoes and in the forests, the same people who survived the death camps, now gather here in the capital of the free world, Washington.

That we the survivors should come, over 15,000 strong, to be together, to remember — and not let others forget.

We remember those days: the terrible loneliness, the utter isolation we felt, abandoned and betrayed by a cold and indifferent world.

We remember the time, just after the war ended, not knowing what had become of our dear ones: our families, our friends and neighbors.

How we were riding trains, placing notes on walls, wandering in the streets, not wanting to believe that all was lost. How we looked into the eyes of strangers and asked, *"Amchu?"* (Are you one of us? Are you, too, a survivor?) This was our password: *"Amchu."*

We could not remain and build our lives on the cemeteries of our dear ones. So we went our separate ways after the war, some to Israel, some to America, some elsewhere. And we *did* rebuild our lives, started new homes, started new families and raised our new generation.

For many of us, those too were lonely years in strange lands.

But although we became proud Americans, we could not separate ourselves from our past.

But sadly, even in our own lifetime, we have come to see the Holocaust denied, taken over and defiled, manipulated and marketed. We have seen the sacred memory of our martyrs distorted and diminished and our six million submerged in a misguided effort to label together all those victims who fell at the hands of the Nazis.

Forty years ago, I had a brother. His name was Mordechai David. He was 17 years old. One day I obtained papers in my name that were thought to guarantee my safe passage out of Poland. A day before my intended departure, my brother begged me for these papers, and I gave them to him. The papers led him to the infamous Hotel Polski in Warsaw and eventually to the trains which took him and others together to the unknown.

It was my name that was listed by the Germans for that transport. By chance I, and not my brother, could have been on that train. Since then, 40 years, I am haunted by the thought that I live my brother's life.

Each of us here has his own story about how he or she suffered and survived. But for a stroke of fate, we were no different from those who perished. We speak in their voice. We speak in their name.

Each of us can tell what he saw, but it is all only a fragment of the vast horror of the Holocaust.

Collectively, however, we can tell the world how we lived and how we resisted. In the words of the prophets, "not by strength, not by force, but by spirit . . ."

Yes, we resisted in Warsaw and other cities, in the camps, in the forests. We defied the Nazis with our will. We taught our children Yiddishkeit and Menschlechkeit in the shadow of the flames.

Only collectively does our legacy make its impact.

Together we can raise a mighty shout to the world, a world bent on repeating the horrors of the past.

We are here.

Mir zeyhen do.

And so the dream began, a dream to gather here in Washington. To be together. To bear witness together. To testify as one in the name of our martyrs.

The world is still not free of the disease which led to Auschwitz and Treblinka. On the streets of Paris and Rome terrorists have slaughtered Jews.

Anti-Semitism now wears the more fashionable cloak of anti-Zionism. In the U.N., Israel is the most reviled of all nations. In the Soviet Union, Jews remain oppressed, and there are new misguided voices that echo the poisonous doctrines of the Nazis.

We still remember the ships with trapped Jews turned back from these shores, the closing door to many refugees, the declining to bomb a railway that led to a death camp. Those are bitter remembrances. But we cannot forget the mighty American army crushing Hitler's Fortress Europa. Tonight, we have assembled here in our nation's capital to give thanks to those hundreds of thousands of young Americans who fought to liberate us and thousands who gave their lives to crush Hitler's Germany. We have come to pay tribute to them and to thank you, America.

Two years ago, many of the same people gathered here, joined other survivors in a World-Gathering of Holocaust survivors in Jerusalem.

Sadly, many of those who gathered there are no longer with us. The days are growing shorter for the survivors. Each week brings news of the death of yet another one of our number. Soon, we the witnesses will all be gone.

But while we are still blessed with life, we must do what we can to see that our past is not forgotten, that our heritage is passed on to our children and to the future generations of the world, that the legacy of our struggle and survival may in turn continue to survive. For this reason, we have come here together with our second generation.

Our sons and daughters will carry forward our legacy of pride, of heroism, of an obligation to keep the memory alive and to warn the world again and again: Don't let this happen again.

And now the vast distance is traversed. We

have come here from all 50 states and Canada, a long and difficult way, separately.

Over the next three days, we will have many opportunities to meet with each other. We shall hope to learn of the fate of our lost loved ones. To join together with the leadership of this country, to share in two glorious cultural events that reach back to our rich roots before the war, to express our close ties to the State of Israel, to witness the transfer of the proposed national memorial to the United States Holocaust Memorial Council — and to tell the world we are here as proud Jews, as remaining survivors and as proud Americans.

From this day forward, no matter where in the world we may be, we the survivors shall always be together.

Forty years, the time it took our ancestors to walk from Egypt into the promised land, have brought us from Warsaw to Washington, from the flames of the Ghetto to the capital of the United States.

And now, my dear friends: Forty years ago, who could have imagined that we, the children of Warsaw or of Lodz, the descendants of scholars and rabbis, of peddlers and poets from Vilna or Vologin, from Vienna or Vitebsk, would have stood in the presence of the president of the United States. Or that I, a child of the Warsaw Ghetto, feeling so terribly alone and angry on this night forty years ago, would have the privilege of introducing the president of the United States to you, my fellow survivors, in the name of all of us.

I have the honor of introducing to you the president of the United States and Mrs. Reagan.

President and Mrs. Reagan
with American Gathering
President Benjamin Meed at
the Capital Centre.

The text of President Reagan's address to the opening ceremony of the American Gathering of Jewish Holocaust Survivors, April 11, 1983.

Thank you very much. President Meed, Chairman Wiesel, the other distinguished leaders of the United States Holocaust Memorial Council, participants in the American gathering of Jewish Holocaust survivors, members of the second generation, friends, survivors — tonight we stand together to give thanks to America for providing freedom and liberty and for many here tonight, a second home and a second life.

The opportunity to join with you this evening as a representative of the people of the United States will be for me a cherished memory. I am proud to accept your thanks on behalf of our fellow Americans and also to express our gratitude to you for choosing America, for being the good citizens that you are and for reminding us of how important it is to remain true to our ideals as individuals and as a nation.

We are here, first and foremost, to remember. These are the Days of Remembrance, *Yom Hashoah.* Ours is the only nation other than Israel that marks this time with an official national observance. For the last two years I've had the privilege of participating personally in the Days of Remembrance Commemoration as President Carter did before me. May we take a moment to pause and contemplate, perhaps in silent prayer, the magnitude of this occasion, the millions of lives, the courage and dignity, the malevolence and hatred, and what it all means to our lives and the decisions that we make more than a generation later. Would you please join me and stand in a tribute to those who are not with us for a moment of silence. [Silent prayer.] Amen.

In the early days of our country, our first president, George Washington, visited a Hebrew congregation in Newport, Rhode Island. In response to their address, he wrote them a now rather famous letter reflecting on the meaning of America's newly won freedom. He wrote, "All possess alike liberty of conscience and immunities of citizenship. For happily the government of the United States, which gives to bigotry no sanction, to persecution no assistance, requires only that they who live under its protection should demean themselves as good citizens." Well, certainly our country doesn't have a spotless record, but our fundamental beliefs, the ones that inspired Washington when he penned that letter, are sound.

Our whole way of life is based on a compact between good and decent people, a voluntary agreement to live here together in freedom, respecting the rights of others and expecting that our rights in return will be respected. But the freedom we enjoy carries with it a tremendous responsibility. You, the survivors of the Holocaust, remind us of that. Good and decent people must not close their eyes to evil, must not ignore the suffering of the innocent — and must never remain silent and inactive in times of moral crisis.

A generation ago the American people felt, like many others in the Western world, that they could simply ignore the expanding power of a totalitarian ideology. Looking back now, we must admit that the warning signs were there that the world refused to see. The words and ideology of the Nazis were rationalized, explained away as if they had no meaning. Violations of religious freedom, the attacks on Jewish property, the censorship, the heavy taxes imposed on those who wished to emigrate, even the first concentration camps — all this ignored, as was the incredible expansion of Germany's war machine.

A few brave voices tried to warn of the danger. Winston Churchill was driven into the political wilderness for speaking the unpleasant truth. There were also those who in their sincere desire for peace were all too ready to give totalitarians every benefit of the doubt and all too quick to label Churchill a warmonger.

Well, time has proven that those who gloss over the brutality of tyrants are no friends of peace or freedom.

Tonight let us pledge that we will never shut our eyes, never refuse to acknowledge the truth, no matter how unpleasant. If nothing else, the painful memory we share should strengthen our resolve to do this. Our Founding Fathers believed in certain self-evident truths, but for truth to prevail we must have the courage to proclaim it.

Last week we reaffirmed our belief in the most meaningful truths of our Judeo-Christian heritage — Passover and Easter. These two religious observances link our faiths and celebrate the liberation of the body and soul. The rights of Passover remind us of the freeing of our common ancestors from the yoke of Pharaoh's bondage and their exodus to freedom. And today you bear witness to a modern-day exodus from the darkness of unspeakable horror to the light and refuge of safe heavens: The two most important being America and what soon became the State of Israel.

As a man whose heart is with you and as president of a people you are now so much a part of, I promise you that the security of your safe haven here and in Israel will never be compromised. Our most sacred task now is ensuring that the memory of this greatest of human tragedies, the Holocaust, never fades; that its lessons are not forgotten. Although so much has been written and said, words somehow are never enough. If a young person, the son or daughter of a neighbor or friend should die or suffer a terrible illness, we feel the sorrow and share the pain. But how can we share the agony of a million young people suffering unspeakable deaths? It's almost too great a burden for the human soul. Indeed, its very enormity may make it seem unreal.

Simon Wiesenthal has said, "When a hundred people die, it's a catastrophe. When a million people die, it's just a statistic."

We must see to it that the immeasurable pain of the Holocaust is not dehumanized, that it is not examined clinically and dispassionately, that its significance is not lost on this generation or any future generation. Though it is now a dry scar, we cannot let the bleeding wound be forgotten.

Only when it is personalized will it be real enough to play a role in the decisions we make. Those victims who cannot be with us today do a vital service to mankind by being remembered. But we must be their vessel of remembrance. This reunion is part of our duty to them.

Ben Meed, by serving as the catalyst for this historic event, you exemplify the meaning of good citizenship. America is lucky to have you. Elie Wiesel, you have done so much for so

many years now, for all you've done, thank you for your noble effort.

Americans can be proud that with the help of these two men and many others, we're moving forward to build a Holocaust Memorial, a living museum here in the nation's capital. And it is being financed, as is this gathering, by voluntary contributions by Jews and gentiles, by citizens from every walk of life, of every race and creed, who grasp the importance to our soul and to our well-being of seeing, of understanding and of remembering.

Imparting the message of the Holocaust, using it to reinforce the moral fiber of our society is much more than a Jewish responsibility. It rests upon all of us who, not immobilized by cynicism and negativism, believe that mankind is capable of greater goodness. For just as the genocide of the Holocaust debased civilization, the outcome of the struggle against those who ran the camps and committed the atrocities gives us hope that the brighter side of the human spirit will, in the end, triumph.

During the dark days when terror reigned on the continent of Europe, there were quiet heroes, men and women whose moral fiber held firm. Some of those are called "Righteous Gentiles." At this solemn time, we remember them also. Alexander Rozlan and his wife, for example, now live in Clearwater, Florida. But during the war, they lived in Poland and they hid three Jewish children in their home for more than four years. They knew the terrible risk they were taking. Once when German soldiers searched their home, the Rozlans kept serving wine and whiskey until the troops were so drunk they forgot what they were looking for. Later, Rozlan's own son, who was in the hospital with scarlet fever, the boy hid half of the medicine under his pillow so he could give it to the Jewish children his family were hiding because they, too, had scarlet fever.

There are many such stories. The picturesque town of Assisi, Italy, sheltered and protected 300 Jews. Father Rufino Niccacci organized the effort, hiding people in his monastery and in the homes of parishioners. A slip of the tongue by a single informant could have condemned the entire village to the camps, yet they did not yield.

And, of course, there was Raoul Wallenberg — one of the moral giants of our time, whose courage saved thousands. He could have remained in his native Sweden, safe from the confligration that engulfed the continent. He chose to follow his conscience. Yes, we remember him, too.

I would affirm, as President of the United States and, if you would permit me, in the names of the survivors, that if those who took him from Budapest would win our trust, let them start by giving us an accounting of Raoul Wallenberg. Wallenberg and others who displayed such bravery did not consider themselves heroes. I understand that some of them when asked about why they risked so much, often for complete strangers, replied, "It was the right thing to do." And that was that. It was just their way.

That kind of moral character, unfortunately, was the exception and not the rule; but for that very reason is a consciousness we must foster.

Earlier, I described our country as a compact between good and decent people. I believe this because it is the love of freedom, not nationalistic rituals and symbols, that unites us. And because of this, we are also bound in spirit to all those who yearn to be free and to live without fear. We are the keepers of the flame of liberty.

I understand that in Hebrew, the word for "engraved" is charut. It is very similar to the word for "freedom," cheyrut. Tonight, we recognize that for freedom to survive and prosper, it must be engraved in our character, so that when confronted with fundamental choices, we will do what is right, because that is our way.

Looking around this room tonight I realize that, although we come from many lands, we share a wealth of common experiences. Many of us remember the time before the Second World War — how we and our friends reacted to certain events has not faded from our memory. There are also in this room many young peple, sons and daughters, maybe even a few grandchildren. Perhaps some of the younger ones can't understand why we're making so much of a fuss. Perhaps some of them think we're absorbed by the heartaches of the past and should move on.

Well, what we do tonight is not for us. It's for them. We who are old enough to remember must make certain those who take our place understand. So, if a youngster should ask you why you are here, just tell that young person — "Because I love God, because I love my country, because I love you, Zachor."

I can't close without remembering something else. Some years ago, I was sent on a mission to Denmark. And while there, I heard stories of the war. And I heard how the order had gone out for the Danish people under the Nazi occupation to identify the Jews among them. And the next day, every Dane appeared on the street wearing a Star of David.

Thank you all. And God bless you.

American Gathering President Benjamin Meed presents a scroll to President and Mrs. Reagan at the Capital Centre in Landover, Md.

TO RISE UP FOR THEIR DIGNITY

BY LAWRENCE MEYER

The most important thing — the dream of my life — has come true. Jewish self-defense in the Warsaw Ghetto has become a fact. Jewish armed resistance and retaliation have been realized. I have been the witness of a splendid, heroic struggle by the Jewish fighters.
— Communication sent by
Mordechai Anielewicz, commandant of
the Jewish Fighting Organization,
from the Warsaw Ghetto, April 23, 1943.

Barbara Steiner, née Bajla Zyskind, was 14 when the Second World War started. She remembers it clearly, along with a great many other things that some people would rather forget.

She was on her way to a store to buy books for school, which would start September 3, 1939. She remembers seeing planes overhead. "I thought, 'They must be ours.' " She was mistaken. The following day, Warsaw was bombed.

We are accustomed now to hearing stories about Jews being randomly, arbitrarily killed by the Germans in World War II, being herded like cattle to the slaughterhouse, being burned like so many million sticks of wood in the ovens.

This story is different. This story is about the time — the first but not the last time — that the Jews fought back.

This month marks the 40th anniversary of the Warsaw Ghetto uprising.

It took a long while for that moment to come — three and a half years. During those years, a world was destroyed, the centuries-old enclaves of Jewish culture and learning in Warsaw, Lvov, Vilna, Riga and hundreds of small villages and towns throughout Europe were leveled. Barbara Steiner, living in Warsaw, watched her family die, leaving her alone at 16.

Before the war, the Zyskind family had been reasonably comfortable. Barbara's father was trained as a rabbi — he was a Hasidic Jew and, therefore, very religious — but he had gone into the family's construction business. Her mother was a housewife. Her two brothers, both older, worked — one was an engineer; the other sold machine parts. The younger brother married in 1938 and his wife had a baby the following year.

The Germans created the Warsaw Ghetto in December 1940, rounding up Jews from various neighborhoods and herding them into one section of the city. The Zyskinds' apartment already had been taken for the German occupation forces in January. Her family was given "15 minutes, maybe half an hour" to pack. "What can you save in 15, 20 minutes?" she asks in heavily accented English that often borrows its sentence construction from Yiddish. "My mother, to her the most precious thing was her wine, which she made. For my father was the books, that was the most precious thing. Whatever we could, we saved, but that was very little. From that time on we were already among the very poor ones, not just poor, but very poor.

We didn't have an apartment. We didn't have where to go. We didn't have any money."

A friend offered a place to live. The entire family moved in, both brothers, wife and child. The Germans built a wall around the ghetto they had created. Food was rationed. "What they gave us and told us we could buy, and what was in the store, wasn't enough to survive," she says. "I'm not talking already to live from it. So the hunger was terrible. There were people dying on the street from starvation." In time, when the starvation worsened, bodies collected in the street and were picked up daily by rickshaws. There were no more horses.

When her own school shut down, Steiner worked for a while teaching smaller children, but then the starvation got too bad, "so people stopped worrying about the children, teaching them and I didn't have what to do."

Her older brother fled when the Gestapo came looking for him after he tried to sell cornmeal he had milled himself. She never saw him again.

Money was scarce, food scarcer. Steiner's father had spent much of his life, she recalls, looking for one volume to complete a set by Moses Maimonides, the physician, theologian and preeminent Jewish philosopher of the Middle Ages. Her father found a copy of the book and bought it with the bread money.

"We are starving. We are hungry," she says, reaching back to re-create the situation from the comfort of a chair in her spacious apartment in Skokie, Illinois. "To him this book was more important than a piece of bread. He said, 'Without the bread, we will somehow survive. But the book,' he said, 'they can take away from you everything, but to take away from you what you have in your mind, they have to kill you.' That was my father. He learned his whole life. He spoke I don't remember how many languages. He was a man with high, high principles of life and extremely, extremely intelligent."

He died of starvation in December 1941. The family could not go to bury him because the cemetery was outside the Ghetto. Steiner's mother died a week after her husband. "I don't think that I cried anymore."

Steiner found another job, caring for a shopkeeper's daughter. "And after a few days I was walking with a sandwich for the little girl. My brother saw me and said, 'Barbara, give me a little piece of bread. I'm dying.' And I didn't. And I never saw him alive again. I lost him a week later. And I was left alone."

Blaming herself now, she stops to weep for a brother dead more than 40 years.

At the time Barbara Steiner's family was dying, Stefan Korbonski and his wife, Zofia, were also living in Warsaw, on the other side of the Ghetto wall, in what he refers to as "the so-called Aryan side." Korbonski was a lawyer, a member of the liberal intelligentsia and one of the leaders of the Polish Underground in

(Top left) The statue of Warsaw Ghetto Uprising leader Mordechai Anielewicz, at Kibbutz Yad Mordechai in Israel.

(Top right) A Nazi cutting the beard of a religious Jew, one of the earlier forms of humiliation practiced by the Germans.

(Above) Barbara Steiner's family before the Holocaust.

(Left) Jewish prisoners being taken from the Warsaw Ghetto.

Warsaw. Throughout the war, he and his wife were active in gathering intelligence, which they radioed to London, and in organizing and directing civil resistance to the German occupation. Korbonski was recognized in 1981 by Yad Vashem, the Holocaust Memorial in Israel, as a "Righteous Gentile," one of those who aided Jews during World War II.

Korbonski, who now lives in a kind of exile with his wife in Washington, dates the beginning of the Holocaust from July 22, 1942. That was the day the Germans announced their intention to transport 7,000 Jews a day from the Ghetto. The Germans said the Jews would resettle in labor camps. In fact, they were taken to Majdanek, a Nazi death camp south of Warsaw.

Korbonski transmitted the information as soon as he learned it. Until then, the BBC had immediately rebroadcast the reports received from Korbonski, he said. No mention was made of the deportations, however. When he demanded to know why, Korbonski said, he received a message: "Not all your radiograms lend themselves to publication." Some time later, he found out, his initial report had been dismissed as exaggerated anti-German propaganda.

In the Ghetto, daily, the Germans were rounding up Jews and taking them to the Umschlagplatz for deportation. The trains left full and returned empty.

For Barbara Steiner, the months after her family's death are a blank. She says she cannot recall what she did, where she lived, how she survived. Her recollection picks up months later. Thousands lay dead in the streets. She was alone. "Dirty, filthy, I was." She sold the lining from her coat for a piece of bread. Someone stole the bread before she could eat it.

To see her today, at 57, a wife and mother of a grown son and daughter, sitting comfortably among the gewgaws and accumulated bric-a-brac of middle-class life, her reddish-blond hair carefully coiffed by professional hands, it is hard to identify this woman with the emaciated girl she describes. How did she survive? She wonders herself.

Physically, she is stout but small, under five feet tall. While serving cakes and cookies with coffee later, she speculates that "the reason we are all fat now is because we didn't have enough to eat then. All the time we thought about food." She cries easily at the memories, but underneath there is the suggestion of strength and determination. She had a will to survive. And, she says, "if I tell you that I thought my father is watching over me and really talked to me, you will think that I am crazy. But that's exactly what happened."

She recalls hearing about a Jewish woman who still had some money and was looking for a young person to care for her daughter. Steiner knew the woman, knocked at her door. She tells this part of the story almost with amusement at how fortune smiles on some and frowns on others with deadly consequences.

"I was terrible filthy. And I suppose she saw some lice crawling. I'm sure. And as she opened the door, she said, 'Barbara, as much as I would love to do, I can't. You're dirty — sickness.' Can you imagine the feeling of a girl? You're talking about a person who's altogether 16 years old. So I cried and walked down. And as I walked down, the Germans were already there because that was already the time that there were actions going on in Warsaw. And what is an action? They close a few streets and they took out all the people which were there."

She dived into a basement through an open window, the Germans firing at her. The basement was full of feathers. She burrowed among them and hid.

When she emerged an hour later, the building was empty. The woman who had turned her down for the job was gone, with everyone else, taken by the Germans. She took some clothes, ate what she could find and went off with another girl who appeared from nowhere to get a slave-labor job at a broom factory in the Ghetto — the only way she could avoid deportation.

The question arises as to why the Jews of the Warsaw Ghetto were so slow to see what was happening. "There is now lots of people asking, 'Why didn't you do anything?' How do you answer?" Steiner ponders her own question. "I tell them, first of all, they did it so systematically. They didn't do it at one time. First of all they took away the furs and the jewelry. So you thought maybe that would be enough. Then they made ghettos. And you figured maybe that would be enough. Then you hungry and you fight for the bread. And mainly, if you take away the dignity from a person, then I don't think so that he's capable of doing a lot."

She recalls one person who escaped from the death camp at Treblinka. "He came to Warsaw and he wasn't completely normal, and he was hollering up the street, and he was saying, 'You're all going to Treblinka. If you're rich or you're poor, you wind up in the same place.' Nobody believed. Nobody believed. First of all, nobody believed because how can a human believe that this is possible. Second of all, if you're terrible hungry, the first thing is how to get food, not how to fight. If it comes to the Orthodox Jew, there was altogether another question about fighting because they believed it was God's will, God will protect them."

In the broom factory where she was working, the Germans came periodically to take people to fill the trains. By now, in the fall and winter of 1942, only the young and strongest were left. Most of the children were gone. The old were gone.

No one knows for sure how many were left of the 500,000 Jews who had lived in Warsaw. Steiner thinks 50,000 remained. "We decided," she said, "that's enough. We will fight. We will not let them slaughter us the same way they did to our parents." Zionist organizations formed fighting units in the Ghetto, as did the Communists and the Jewish Bund. The most famous of these fighters was Mordechai Anielewicz, a young student — "skinny," Steiner remembers, the son of a couple who owned a fruit store, not the type one would think of as a leader at all. She remembers him as a "very shy boy." He was a member of the left-wing group Hashomer Hatzair, the Young Guard.

The Jews of the Ghetto learned how to make Molotov cocktails. They were taught how to use weapons. Steiner was recruited at age 17 to be a nurse. She was assigned a bunker, designated by the street address 30 Swientojerska. She was not permitted to visit it until the uprising began.

Arms were purchased and smuggled in by Jews who managed to pass as Gentiles on the "Aryan" side of the wall. The Polish Underground provided some arms, not nearly enough in the estimation of the Jews who survived the uprising.

On January 18, 1943, the fighters confronted the Germans in some relatively small incidents, inflicting some casualties and suffering some.

In April, as Passover approached, rumors started circulating in and out of the Ghetto that

In December 1940, the Germans built a wall around an area that they set aside for Jews from Warsaw and elsewhere. In April 1943, after the Germans had transported hundreds of thousands of Jews from that Ghetto to their deaths in extermination camps, the remaining Jews took up arms against the Germans, who retaliated by burning the Ghetto and later leveling it.

a mass deportation was coming. Steiner recalls that it was quiet in the Ghetto. The word was that when the special squads surrounded the Ghetto and came in, the uprising would start.

It began April 19, when the first forces entered the deserted streets of the Ghetto. Steiner recalls that she was setting the table for the Passover seder when she was told to go to her bunker. As the Germans and their support entered the Ghetto, they were met with gunfire.

Korbonski recalls with pride that he immediately sent a message to London announcing the uprising and pleading for the British to address the Ghetto fighters from a secret radio station called Swit (Daybreak) that the British had set up in London. They tried to give the impression that it was located in Poland.

The British complied. In his memoirs, Korbonski recalls listening to one such broadcast, "a program based on our telegram, designed to make it seem as if the announcer were describing his impressions as he looked out from the window of the radio station, and saw the blaze and smoke and heard the roar of cannon . . . We looked at each other, feeling a kind of sorrowful satisfaction."

Knowing they had almost no chance of success, Steiner says, they still hoped. "We were hoping that maybe a miracle will happen — that maybe the war will end in between. Maybe they will open a front and they will start to bombing Warsaw and even to bombing the Ghetto with us. But just to destroy the Germans . . . But most of all, the hope was to see revenge. In that time, I did want to survive, I really did. From '43, I did not see that it will be possible for me to survive, so at least to kill a few Germans. At least to do something."

The fighting raged for weeks. The Germans estimated their casualties at 16 dead and 85 wounded. The ghetto fighters estimated 1,000 German dead and wounded. From historical accounts of the fighting, the higher figure seems more accurate.

Her bunker, Steiner recalls, held about 50 people. Although some bunkers were cramped and overcrowded, Steiner remembers hers as being large with enough supplies to last a year. They had food, a well for water, electricity and communications with a lookout in the building. Every night, when the Germans pulled back from the Ghetto, there was a patrol. Steiner went on one such patrol, on eerily quiet, deserted streets. Whoever did not know the countersign when challenged was to be shot.

They would have lasted longer, Steiner maintains, except that the Germans started burning the buildings. Stukas bombed the Ghetto from the air, the Germans shelled the buildings and soldiers torched them. Steiner never had a chance to use her nursing training. "There was nobody wounded. They were dead, because a German didn't leave anybody wounded. We thought that we'd really be able to face the Germans, but we weren't. They were killing us and making sure that we were dead. There wasn't even one wounded.

"Now that I think about it, I didn't use even one Band-Aid. Nothing."

Steiner was among a handful who managed to escape the bunker at Swientojerska 30 to another nearby. Some were killed by poison gas; others were shot or perished in the flames. The Germans found Steiner's second bunker on May 5, 1943. She was shipped off with the others to Majdanek in a cattle car whose windows had been boarded shut to provide as little air as possible. Steiner survived by breathing through

a knothole for three days. She recalls that at least half of the 150 or more people in her car were dead when the train arrived at Lublin.

On May 8, the Germans surrounded the main bunker at Mila 18, where Anielewicz and the other leaders of the Jewish Fighting Organization had their headquarters. About 300 civilians surrendered. The 80 fighters inside refused to come out. The Germans used poison gas. Some of the fighters committed suicide. It is said that before they died, each sang the song of his party or group. Anielewicz was among those who died. Today, a memorial to him stands at a border kibbutz in Israel named for him. The statue of Anielewicz is of heroic proportions.

The Germans claimed that the fighting was over by May 16, after four weeks — longer than it took the Wehrmacht to defeat the Polish Army, Steiner notes with pride. In fact, the fighting lasted longer. Shots were reported as late as September in the Ghetto. Fresh traces of fighters were found in a bunker in October. The Germans leveled the Ghetto, but Jews survived in caves until the Polish uprising in August 1944.

The motivation behind the uprising was simple, according to Steiner: "It wasn't a question of survival. It was a question to die with dignity. To show the world that we are not animals, that they could not do what they did to everybody. That was the main reason . . . This was for our fathers, for our mothers, for the whole families. That was exactly our feeling. We told ourselves that we will fight to the end. And we would have if it wouldn't have been for the fire."

What she regrets is that the uprising did not occur earlier. "I wish that it would have happened before. I wish that we wouldn't wait until '43. I wish we could have started it in '39 when there was a half a million. If each one of us would take one stone, we would kill them by the thousands. And then I think I'm proud of what we did."

At that time, Steiner worried about what kind of person she would be if she survived:

"If I talk about everything I went through, I'm not talking about me, *me*. Because I wouldn't be able to go through everything and still be normal — quote unquote normal, whatever that means. I'm talking like two different people. This other person, this *other* Barbara, went through all those things, I didn't. *I* didn't. Because how can you after such a cataclysm, such a destruction of everything, how can you raise children? How can you laugh? How can you enjoy a normal life?

"And how can you want to achieve yet some things in life, like in our case we came to this country and most of us didn't have anything. We had to learn the language, what little we know. We had to build our life. We had to start from a knife and a fork and a spoon, and never ask for charity. I would die before I would ask for charity. So, this couldn't be the same person. I suppose this blocks out, my mind blocks out this part.

"I was always afraid what kind of a person I would come out after the war, if I was all right. Because I was afraid I would come out without a feeling, you know what I mean? The minute the war stopped, it was the same. I can cry with a baby. I can cry with a movie . . . I am a believer — with everything. I'm a big believer in God. If you don't believe, it's a terrible empty space. And I have so many empty spaces that I have to have something.

"Yes, I am," she adds wistfully, as an afterthought. "That's funny, but I am."

It took the German Army more than a month to subdue the Warsaw Ghetto Uprising, despite the use of aerial bombardment, artillery and tanks to fight the remaining inhabitants. The Ghetto fighters were armed only with light weapons, Molotov cocktails and other home-made explosives. When captured, the Ghetto fighters were marched to a collection point and taken to concentration camps.

LOOKING FOR FACES, WATCHING THE SIGNS, AND ALWAYS HOPING

BY CARLA HALL

> **My father was a lumber and furniture manufacturer. He bribed people to get us false papers and to hide us in the homes of Gentiles. I went to Protestant schools. I was an altar boy. We were betrayed by the daughter of the people that were hiding us. She wasn't mad at us. She wanted money; it was strictly business. She was paid much less than 30 pieces of silver.**

Mark Rubin, 46, Beverly Hills banker.
Born in Sabinov, Czechoslovakia.
Imprisoned at Theresienstadt.

Eva Kor has propped up her sign on a table. It is a little island of space in the caverns of the Washington Convention Center where 10,000 survivors of the Holocaust have gathered. She was 10 when she went to Birkenau with her twin sister, Miriam, and became a subject for the barbaric Dr. Josef Mengele. She was liberated three days before her 11th birthday. Her sister, Miriam, lives in Israel now.

Eva Kor is 49 with short brown hair and an animated German-accented voice. She carries a dog-eared typewritten copy of her memoirs, "Nothing But the Will to Live," which she eagerly shares with visitors.

"I would love to be able to meet somebody else who was there. Some of the things that happened are so foggy, I'd love to verify whether they were true as I remember them. There were several kinds of experiments. They would do psychological experiments where they would take us to Auschwitz, take off our clothes and watch our behavior for six or seven hours. And there were the experiments in the lab. They would take blood [from twins] — they had huge vials for it — and inject it into [gentile, German] women to see if they would have twins. You see, Dr. Mengele wanted the Aryan race to multiply."

She wears a brown pantsuit and fashionably tinted glasses. "This is what I remember," she says, her voice intense and agitated. "I've never heard it from anyone else. I'd like to hear it from someone else."

A minute later, a woman walks by and pauses to examine Kor's sign, squinting a little at the words. A faint smile comes across her face. "Are you from the twins?" she asks.

"Yes," says Kor. "Were you at Birkenau?" The woman nods.

"What do you remember about the twins?" asks Kor.

"I saw some of the twins," says Frieda Knoll Bassman, 64. "They took the blood from them . . ."

Kor gasps a little and her arms reach out toward Bassman.

". . . until they died," finishes Bassman.

"Yes," says Kor, nodding, "some of them died."

Bassman sits down next to her. "I thought all the twins died," says Bassman with a smile, patting Kor's hand. "You were one of the lucky ones. I used to jump over a fence and bring them water. They were so thirsty."

Bassman lives in Chicago now, Kor in Terre Haute, Indiana. Bassman again looks at Kor, a smile of amazement spreading across her face. "I'm so happy to meet you," she says, putting an arm around Kor. "I thought no twins had survived."

Among 10,000 survivors of the Holocaust some extraordinary reunions occurred. But mostly, they didn't occur. People searched, bearing their own names or those of lost

friends and relatives on their T-shirts, on large pieces of paper stuck in their hats or pinned to the backs of their blouses and shirts:

HAVE YOU SEEN
MY SISTER
HENA MILICH?
FROM
LODZ

Esther Milich Kozminski, from Beverly Hills, wore those red letters on her sweatshirt, looking for the sister she has not seen since 1940. She didn't find her sister but she found another woman at the gathering named Esther Milich. "I took out my checkbook and it said, 'Esther Milich'; she took out hers and it said, 'Esther Milich,' " she says smiling. "We exchanged addresses. Why not?"

Over an Indian cotton blouse and full skirt, Mona Baum, 23, wears her small billboard sign around her neck with the word "Auschwitz" painted on, dripping red. An old photo of a young man is pasted on with the following message: "This is My Father. He is alive and well. We are looking for his sister, Adel Elbaum." The billboard originally was for her father to wear, but he slipped a disc and could not attend the gathering.

BARUCH A. LIEBER
BORN — NOWY SANCZ
KRAKOW, POLAND
BUCHENWALD — GROS ROSEN

The sign wraps around Lieber's straw hat. It attracts the attention of a network television crew and draws the anger of a convention attendee who walks by and declares hotly, "This man wants to be on television." The angered man is scolded by relatives who pull him away.

Anna Maria Smulowitz also spied Lieber. "I went up to him and said, 'Did you know my father?' He just put his hand on my arm and said, 'I wish I had.' " She blinks back the tears. "I have this heavy fantasy that I'm going to find someone here," she said. Her father, now dead, was a Buchenwald survivor. "He had 10 brothers and sisters that we never knew about, because he never talked. He told me nothing."

PAULA
KEMPINSKI
KOLO
POLAND

"I went all out," says Kempinski, an Auschwitz survivor, of her white T-shirt with big black letters. "I said if this doesn't work, forget it."

Sometimes survivors leave urgent but discreet notes at the message center. Regina Spiegel of Silver Spring unfolds one left for her husband, Sam, to find a printed message: *"I hope you are the son of Mr. Spiegel who sold shoes to my father, Jozef Krim in Lwow. Please call."* It is signed by a survivor.

"It's unbelievable," says Spiegel.

Only an hour earlier, Sam Spiegel and several of his friends ran into each other —

they had last been together shortly after the liberation of the camps. There was a great jumble of hugging and kissing and exclamations reminiscent of school reunions. Spiegel put one arm around Max Weizman and one arm around Saul Flame. "We were in camp together," he said proudly, grinning. It was Auschwitz.

"I hadn't seen this guy in 30 years," Flame said of Spiegel. "But I know him — same face."

Bella Bialkowicz has tears in her eyes as each of her friends hugs her.

"I worked in the kitchen; I used to cook soup," she says of the labor camp, Pionki, where she was.

"But she knew us, so she gave us more," Weizman says with a grin, putting an arm around her.

"I used to go out and steal the potatoes to put in the soup so there would be more for everyone," Bialkowicz says, laughing.

Her daughter Susan watches, smiling and crying softly. "We were looking all day for this," she says, "looking in people's faces . . ."

(Above) Sam Shatz of Brooklyn breaks into tears as he recounts his life in one of Hitler's death camps. (Below) Moments after a ceremony at Arlington honoring the men who died while attempting to free prisoners of the Nazis.

EVIL HISTORY, PAINFUL STORIES

BY JUDY MANN

Anita Epstein was born in the Krakow ghetto. Her mother gave her away when she was three months old to a Gentile woman who had four children of her own, to be raised as a Catholic. "They realized — most of them — they were going into camps," Epstein recalls. "Whether they realized babies were going to be thrown off roofs . . . " Most of her immediate family, including grandparents, aunts and two young cousins, perished in the camps. Her mother survived Auschwitz.

After the war she returned to Krakow and found her daughter. They came to the United States when Anita was nine and settled in New York. "Living in New York," she says, "you somehow knew about it . . . In my house, people talked about it constantly." The choice that author William Styron's Sophie had to make in Auschwitz — "that surrounded me all my life," says Epstein.

Then she moved to Washington, or more to the point, away from New York. Twice in recent years she has encountered adult, college-educated Americans who had never heard about the Holocaust. "The same thing happened to my daughter," she says. "When the *Holocaust* [television program] was shown, she went to school — in that school there were only three or four Jews — several kids said we had no idea this ever existed." Lucy S. Dawidowicz, author of *The War Against the Jews* and *The Holocaust and the Historians*, writes in the latter: "It is plain from even the most cursory review of textbooks and scholarly works by English and American historians that the awesome events of the Holocaust have not been given their historic due. For over two decades some secondary school and college texts never mentioned the subject at all, while others treated it so summarily or vaguely as to fail to convey sufficient information about the events themselves or their historical significance."

She attributes this partly to academic training that leads American historians to specialize and partly to the American taste for the pragmatic over the ideological. "The Holocaust and Nazism and its anti-Semitism and racism was fundamentally an ideological question. It was a world view."

Anita Epstein is the wife of a colleague and friend. I remember being stunned to discover that the wife of a friend and contemporary had been so intimately affected by the concentration camps of Nazi Europe. On a different scale, others of my generation and younger have been surprised to discover recently that 100,000 Americans of Japanese descent were interned in camps by the American government.

The 20th century has produced violence and human carnage on a scale unprecedented in the history of man. Richard L. Rubenstein, in *The Cunning of History*, cites estimates of 100 million people being killed during this century as a direct result of political acts by states. The least helpful way to view the Holocaust, he argues, is as the work of a handful of demented criminals. The Jews of Europe were regarded by many nations, not just the Germans, as surplus people, he notes. "At Auschwitz," he writes, "the Germans revealed new potentialities in the human ability to dominate, enslave and exterminate. They also revealed new areas in which capitalistic enterprise might profitably and even respectably be employed. The camps were thus far more of a permanent threat to the human future than they would have been had they functioned solely as an exercise in mass killing." He warns of how this could become the prototype of a future social order, "especially in a world confronted by catastrophic crises and ever-increasing, massive population redundancy."

On the front of the National Archives is inscribed the saying: "The Past Is Prologue." Yet we, as a nation, teach precious little about it. We learn about slavery from a television series. We graduate people from high school who have only a vague idea of the Nazi extermination program.

It is because of this that some 10,000 survivors of concentration camps felt compelled to gather in Washington to remind the rest of America of the Holocaust. Their stories are so painful to read one wonders how they can even speak of what happened. They did so because they understand that it is not enough to be silent or to speak only among themselves or with their families. They understand the lack of a sense of history that Americans have. They know that a nation that does not study and understand evil in the past is ill-equipped to prevent it in the future.

THE CHILDREN: INHERITORS OF A PAINFUL LEGACY

BY NEIL HENRY

Until two summers ago, Jeanette Binstock knew very little about what really happened to her family in Poland during World War II. The 31-year-old Gaithersburg woman, a daughter of immigrant parents, said she enjoyed an innocent childhood in New York, knowing only bits and pieces of the story.

Then in 1980, when her mother died after spending the last 20 years of her life in a New York mental hospital, Binstock and her two brothers gathered at the family home in Queens to sit shiva, the traditional seven-day Jewish period of mourning.

It was then, in detail, that her father began to recount the family's European horror.

He told how the Nazis came in 1939 and herded the Jews into ghettos and cattle cars. He told how Binstock's mother had suffered a bullet wound in the back trying to escape, how a Nazi soldier had tried to rape her and how the trauma led to a later emotional collapse.

He described how each of her mother's relatives was murdered in the war, by gas and guns, and how nearly everyone in his own family was machine-gunned to death one afternoon in a forest outside the town of Drogobych.

"It was the first time my father really talked to us about the war. By the time he finished I had this intense feeling for relatives I'd never seen," Binstock recalled. "I was overwhelmed by the courage of my mother. She was someone I had never really known."

Binstock, a budget analyst for the U.S. Department of Education, took time to participate in seminars sponsored by the American Gathering of Jewish Holocaust Survivors. She was joined by 4,000 others who came from around the country and share with her a desire to remember the legacy of European forebears they never had a chance to know.

They are the second generation: American children of Jewish Holocaust survivors.

They met at the Washington Convention Center to attend often-emotional workshops and discussions organized by second-generation members. The topics included "Creative Responses to the Holocaust" and "Integration of Survivor Children into Society." At times the discussions, attended by overflow crowds, turned into passionate political arguments between the children and their surviving parents.

At one point political scientist Jerzy Warman, a Polish-born child of survivors, pleaded for support of the Solidarity movement in Poland. He was drowned out by vehement protests from many elderly survivors of the Holocaust in Poland who condemned Polish Gentiles for aiding the Nazis during World War II and charged that anti-Semitism there continues to this day.

At another point, in a discussion of Holocaust art, a young Jewish art historian,

speaking of Nazi war atrocities, was interrupted by an elderly survivor in the back of the crowd. Attempting to correct her, the survivor shouted, "It was the Germans! The Germans! Not just the Nazis!" before leaving the room in anger.

The drama and moving personal accounts that unfolded at the convention center pointed to the complex and dynamic moral and political questions that second-generation members are beginning to grapple with as they accept, in young adulthood, the legacy of their parents.

They include people like Binstock, who is now attemping to pass the legacy on to her own children, and Mark Tykocinski, an immunologist and genetic engineering researcher at the National Institutes of Health, who, aware of crude Nazi research in a similar field, each day confronts moral questions relating to his work.

As Yale University film professor Annette Insdorf, also a child of survivors, put it yesterday, "We simply don't have the luxury of forgetfulness."

There are about 250,000 children of survivors in North America. Most are in their thirties now, pursuing careers in many walks of life and raising families of their own.

They are as heterogenous a group as their parents. Some are devout followers of the faith, while others are less so and fully assimilated into the melting pot. Some are middle-class housewives, grocers and Vietnam veterans, while still others are highly successful in business, politics and science — forging an American Dream from a catastrophe only a generation ago.

They all share, however, the legacy of survival.

They were born after the war to parents who endured the barbarity of the Nazi regime, who hid out in basements and haystacks, joined partisan resistance fighters and were among the few survivors of the concentration camps.

They were brought up in the security of American homes, knowing nonetheless that many of their relatives had been murdered only a few years before they were born.

And eventually, through word of mouth, old photographs and occasional signs such as tears at Yom Kippur, they learned of their parents' pre-World War European way of life and the atrocities that destroyed it.

As recently as 10 years ago, it would have been unlikely to hear topics at the convention center raised, much less discussed. Only within the last few years, largely through the research work of a few psychotherapists and psychologists and a New York journalist named Helen Epstein, have children of survivors come to recognize themselves as a distinct social group.

"What binds them together is a need to have continuity with the past. It has to do with the process of mourning. They have a need to mourn their grandparents, aunts and uncles,"

(Top) On arrival at Auschwitz en route directly to the gas chambers. (Above left) Children in the Warsaw Ghetto: tired, tattered, hungry. (Above right) A survivor of Buchenwald, Moniek Riff, seeks a reunion with old friends.

said Eva Fogelman, a doctoral candidate in psychology at the City University of New York, who has done extensive counseling work with children of survivors and investigated how their lives have been shaped by their parents' experiences of persecution.

Reared in the United States, many children of survivors quickly assumed American cultural values, Fogelman said, without having much of a chance to integrate their ancestors' experiences into their own lives.

To some survivors there was a stigma attached in the Jewish community to being a survivor. "The implication was that they had done something wrong to live through it," Fogelman said.

Others settled in areas where there weren't many Jews. "In both cases," Fogelman went on, "there was, for some, a sense of being cut off from the past and feeling adrift."

In 1979 Epstein, a 35-year-old child of Czechoslovak survivors, wrote a best-seller titled *Children of the Holocaust — Conversations with Sons and Daughters of Survivors*. It was a poignant account of Epstein's travels around the United States, Canada and Israel in search of children of survivors who, like her, had struggled to find a way to come to terms with their parents' ordeal.

Among others, she found one man who fought in Vietnam to prove that he, like his parents, could survive terror and war; and a troubled young Jewish woman who had attended schools in South America with children of former Nazis and was reared as a Christian by her parents after they severed all ties to Judaism.

The book, coupled with accounts of revisionist history put forth by extremists who declared that the Holocaust was a "myth," triggered the formation of a number of political and social action groups made up of children of survivors.

Today there are hundreds of such groups around the country, including the 275-member, Washington-based Generation After, which meets monthly at the Jewish Community Center in Rockville for public discussions of the Holocaust.

"Our presence in Washington is more than just a symbolic act," said Menachem Z. Rosensaft, a New York lawyer and chairman of the International Network of Children of Jewish Holocaust Survivors, a social action organization with 35 affiliated groups in North America and Israel.

"We are committed to commemorating the Holocaust and ensuring that it doesn't happen again — not only to Jews, but to anyone else. That's the legacy we must accept."

Epstein concurs. "It's important to emphasize the cross-cultural aspects," she said. "The Japanese at Hiroshima, black people facing racial injustice here, the experience of Cambodian immigrants — it's all about trauma and how one goes about facing losses and repairing injuries to self-esteem."

Acceptance of the legacy has come in various ways. In Washington the second generation includes Rep. Samuel Gejdenson (D-Conn.), whose Lithuanian parents emigrated to America in the late 1940s. Most of his parents' relatives, including his mother's first husband and child, perished in the war.

Reared on a dairy farm in Bozrah, Connecticut, Gejdenson said the Holocaust was discussed very little in his home, and when it was, his parents would speak in Yiddish in order not to frighten him with the accounts.

One of Gejdenson's earliest childhood memories is of a group of local children who gathered at a neighbor's home in Bozrah one day and asked a woman there where the Gejdensons had come from and why they spoke such a strange language.

The woman told the children that their new neighbors were "from the Old Testament." Gejdenson recalled that the children were awed to learn that a people 5,000 years old could possibly still be alive.

To Gejdenson, the legacy has come to mean political involvement. "When I was 13 or 14 there were some difficult emotional adjustments, knowing what went on over there. But once you deal with that frightening occurrence, you end up a stronger person."

The second generation also includes Tykocinski, the 31-year-old research scientist at NIH, who said he feels "much more hatred toward the perpetrators" of the Holocaust than his parents ever did.

"If Klaus Barbie were in my living room I could quite easily do something that my father couldn't," said Tykocinski, whose father survived Auschwitz and whose mother was liberated from Bergen-Belsen.

"Throughout everything, my father never lost his sense of humanity. He said he never had a desire to pick up a gun."

As a researcher in immunology and recombinant DNA technology, Tykocinski said he is "naturally sensitized" to moral questions relating to his work because he is a child of survivors.

"The Nazis performed research vaguely relating to what I'm doing now, though in a much more brutal way," he said. "I simply can't avoid contending with ethical and moral questions every day I live."

Another child of survivors, 31-year-old Arlington television producer Michael Kornblit, encountered anti-Semitism in his hometown of Ponca City, Oklahoma, where his Polish-born father and mother, who survived Auschwitz, settled after the war.

Bruised and bloodied after fights with other youths who taunted him, Kornblit always lied to his parents about how he suffered his wounds in order to protect them from a recurrence of memories of the war.

"They went through so much [in Europe] that the last thing they needed was to think it could happen here as well," he said.

To Kornblit, the legacy means working to preserve the past. Several years ago he compiled an oral history of the Holocaust experiences of his parents, who were childhood sweethearts before the war and survived separations, harrowing escapes from Nazi soldiers and periods in labor camps, to be reunited and married when the terror was over.

Kornblit's research eventually led him to Newcastle, England, where last year he found a surviving brother of his mother, who she thought had perished at Auschwitz. Last year the brother and sister were reunited here after a 40-year separation.

And the second generation includes Jeanette Binstock, who after listening to her father's story for the first time two summers ago, today feels infused by a new and more profound sense of identity. "Before, I wondered how and if I should tell my children about the war," she says. "Now that I really know what happened, it's a matter of necessity. I have to tell them. It's something you just can't let people forget."

(Top) These Warsaw boys and girls organized a choir, despite the oppression and starvation of the Ghetto. (Left) Michael Korenblit with his parents, Manya and Meyer, survivors of the Holocaust.

SURVIVING THE HOLOCAUST

BY CHARLES FENYVESI

At night I fight back. But the Nazis are again more numerous, and once more I am a child on the run — with forged papers, another identity. Capture is a matter of time. Death is a release — what else can they do to me? Besides, after nearly 40 years, the nightmare is familiar. But will it ever go away? Am I stuck with the memory for the rest of my life?

When will I overcome my anger with my children for leaving food on their plates? Will I stop resenting people who never knew real hunger — that dull nonstop toothache in the stomach? And, damn it, must a wisp of smoke from the far end of a lovely meadow remind me of the crematoria?

I must not react to individuals I dislike with conjectures about how they might behave if ordered to shoot people. Even for a moment it's ridiculous to think of my best Gentile friends as the kind of people who, if such a need ever arose, would surely hide my family in their attics. I didn't choose them as friends because of that. Or maybe I did. I prefer heroes and other crazies to sober bookkeepers.

As a reporter, 75 percent of my job is listening. Patiently, objectively. Writing a story on the Pentagon shipping back Nazi war art to Bonn is just another assignment. The war is over. I don't wince when crowds of demonstrators shout "Hitler" or "Sieg Heil" at Lyndon Johnson or Richard Nixon or Ronald Reagan. This is another continent, another generation — a new world. The swastika is recycled as a punk button; Auschwitz is a metaphor. And Holocaust is a series on TV.

I am as courteous as my colleague, a southern gentleman, when at 9 in the evening, a stranger insists on reading on the telephone long excerpts from her epic poem on Auschwitz. It is in Hungarian, my mother language and hers. In one neat couplet after the other, she mourns her twin babies. I ask about her son who is alive, here and now. She cites her duty to remember — and mine.

I repress an urge to shout, "Shut up, already" in the White House press room when Menachem Begin toasts an American president with a 15-minute lecture on the meaning of the Holocaust. Can the slaughter in Europe of six million men, women and children be the factor in deciding policy on the West Bank of the Jordan River? Must every thought of compromise conjure up the ghost of appeasement in Munich?

We all strike our own bargains. In the spring of 1944, in the provincial Hungarian town of Debrecen, my mother offered God a deal: She would keep the Jewish law only if her mother came back alive. My grandmother didn't return from Auschwitz, and my mother stopped saying her prayers and declared the dietary laws null and void. When ordered to wear the six-pointed star of shame, my father, never before much of a Jew, took me for a walk through the neighborhood to parade our pride in the Star of David, made of the finest, brightest golden velvet.

The trick is to remember *and* to forget, to continue to start anew. I come from a particular family; I exult in our resemblances. Who would I be without calling the roll of relatives burned, hanged, shot? Each time my wife gave birth, I heard them whisper, "Everything will be all right." I kept thinking that my grandmother prompted my son at his bar mitzvah.

The Talmud rules that if a funeral procession runs into a wedding party the wedding party has the right of way. I am in both assemblies.

The author (right) and cousin, Kati Schwarcz, in 1941 in Debrecen, Hungary. She was killed in Auschwitz in June 1944.

As the Nazis tightened their grip inside Germany and later elsewhere, Jews were subjected to public humiliation (left), only a prelude to harsher measures to come. (Top) Jewish women are formed up in ranks outside a barracks at Auschwitz; behind them, the kitchen chimneys of the Hungarian women's camp.

FIVE SURVIVORS AND THEIR FAITHS

BY PAULA HERBUT

Rosa Blum, from Hungarian Rumania, now 54 and living in Dallas, Tex., was 14 when she was taken to Auschwitz. "I was an Orthodox Jew in a very Orthodox home. I remember [in Auschwitz] when Passover came, the first day I didn't eat nothing that day, because you're supposed to eat matzo. So I just fasted that day to observe . . .

"I did ask how can this happen. One night, it was Yom Kippur night, and the Germans used to be very, very, cruel — they used to do cruel things on the Jewish holidays. In 1944, in Auschwitz, I was working in the kitchen the night before Yom Kippur. In the middle of the night, they threw a curfew, a complete, silent curfew. And the black cars arrived, and they took all the children out of the children's block.

"They had loaded all the children into this block, fed them better, gave them cream of wheat, milk. And then that night, they came in with little black cars and took them all to the crematorium, a couple hundred children. And as they were going out the children were chanting the memorial chant, 'Hear, O Israel, the Lord Our God is one . . .

"That's when I was questioning it and I still question it today. How can You do it? Why did You do it? I fought Him. But right away I ask for forgiveness.

"Before this whole thing happened, my grandmother told me about a dream she had, and that dream helped me very much. I have not revealed it to anyone since. She told me she dreamed a dream, that she had seen that God had pulled a black scarf on the heaven, that he would not see the screams of the Jewish people. And each time things happened very hard on me, it helped me. I said, God, put a hole into the scarf, your curtain, and let the screams come through.

"I keep a kosher house in my home, I keep it up. It's something my family kept."

"WE CANNOT LIVE WITHOUT GOD"

Sigmund Strochlitz, 66, from Bendzin, Poland, now a businessman living in New London, Conn., and chairman of the United States Holocaust Memorial Council's Days of Remembrance Committee, was in three concentration camps for two and a half years: Auschwitz, Stuthof and Bergen-Belsen.

"I have seen human beings in Auschwitz who came and were deeply religious before, losing faith and defying and challenging their past, and on the contrary, people who were atheists who went with me to schools and were mocking God, and coming to Auschwitz, becoming great believers.

"Many times I was thinking that perhaps those that were atheists coming to that hell, perhaps were blaming themselves for the tragedies by denying God, while those who strongly believed in the existence of an omnipotent, protecting God see children being thrown into ditches and fire, that their world broke down for them, their belief and their faith were shattered. This is an explanation that a layman could give, and based on my personal observance.

"I was not a very religious human being, [but] a human being who couldn't understand that there are human beings in this world who could go in the morning to church, and play in the day with their children, and be fathers and husbands, and go every day to work knowing in advance that their work means just killing innocent people that they have never met before, and doing it perhaps even with relish, SS men. And when after the war I found out that many of them were highly educated people — professors and doctors, and even theologians — this was my disbelief.

"We cannot live without God, and it is difficult to live with the existence of a compassionate God after [the Holocaust].

"I raised my children in the belief and to have faith. I have a very traditional home. All the holidays are being kept. They're mainly kept with the historical aspect being underlined. I feel that this gives them identity and rules. It develops in them a very strong feeling for the Jewish people and their responsibility to each other. It's a traditional home with a love for our people, and for mankind."

"I NEVER DID DOUBT GOD"

Max Glauben, 52, of Dallas, Tex., is vice president of a plastics extrusion company. He was born in Warsaw and from 1940 to 1943, he was in the Warsaw Ghetto; from 1943 to 1945, he was in four concentration camps.

"I didn't lose my faith. The Holocaust strengthened my faith in God. I felt when I wanted to pray to Him, I could get to Him. I always thought never to question the power of God. Just the fact that I'm here is a sign He must have been good to me.

"The first camp, Majdanek, was a gas chamber. My mother and little brother perished. The next, Budzyn, was a concentration camp. My father was beaten to death. Because three people escaped, they punished 30 people.

"I was only 15 years old when I was liberated. I was denied my youth. I was denied my religion. Being forbidden religion, I believed it more, and it was strengthened in me. Our only hope was the unknown, and that was God.

"I was always taught as a child not to doubt God, and I never did doubt God. I was raised in an Orthodox home. My father owned an Orthodox newspaper in Warsaw. I was 13 years old when I went into the camp.

"I truly did not believe that God with His power did the horrible things of the Holocaust. I think people did them. He permitted them only in a matter of speaking. He provides us

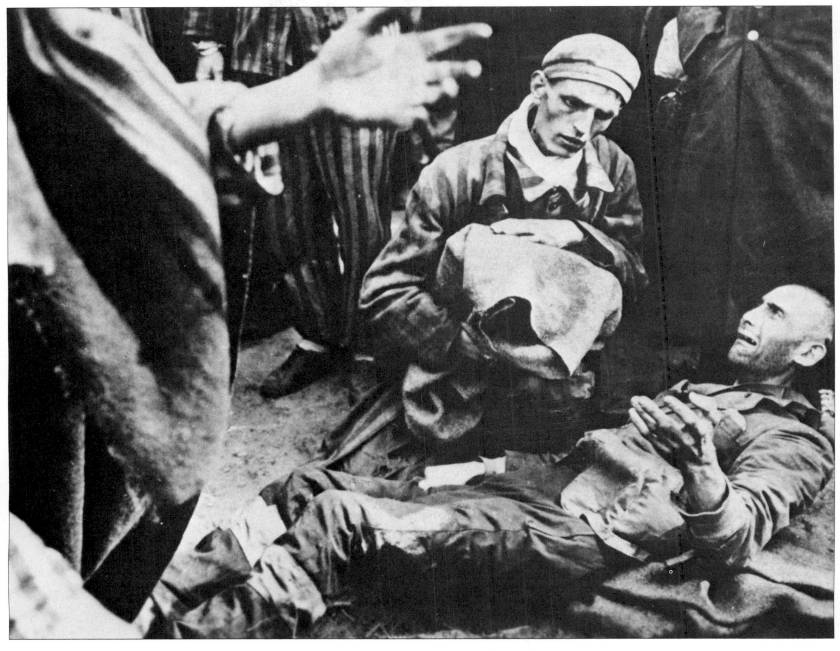

Those who survived Nazi persecution and concentration-camp life
showed the effects of starvation and slave-labor conditions.
(Top) Survivors of the Wobbelin concentration camp shortly after its liberation in 1945.
(Left) American soldiers who liberated Buchenwald found thousands of unburied dead
in the buildings and on the ground. German civilians, who claimed ignorance of what
had happened inside the camps, were conscripted by the Allies to bury the dead.
(Right) The commandant of the Landsberg camp in Germany amid the bodies of some of the
prisoners who died there. The picture was made after the U.S. Seventh Army entered.

with the power of living, creation, destruction. I think He gives us these powers and says, you do them with the best of your ability. I think the people are abusing God's powers that He gave to them."

"IT WAS AN UNMERCIFUL GOD"

Isaac Aron, 69, is a retired businessman from Brooklyn, N.Y., and author of a book on the Holocaust, *Fallen Leaves*. He was raised in a small Polish town near Vilna, now the capital of Lithuania, and fought with the partisans during the war.

"I felt why God permit this crime for innocent people, that children, women, and men should be destroyed in such a terrible way without judgment, without investigation. I felt depressed, hurt inside, and always with doubt and questioning why God permit this crime. Not losing my faith in God, but still doubt in God's judgment, no doubt in His existence, but in the way He allowed this terrible happenings. This is something I couldn't understand. It always bothers my mind. I couldn't get over it, because I lost my family, I lost my parents, two sisters and all my uncles, their children, my friends.

"The German SS, with the help of the local police, made a grave in the wooded section around our village and divided the population in groups and took them to the grave and killed them, children, women, and even sick.

"They took the groups to the grave on the excuse of checking the documentation. They took groups and brought them to the wooded section and there was prepared a grave, and a board was over the middle of the grave. Groups of 10 were told to undress, because they wanted to keep the clothes, they did not want bullet holes, and they shot them, and they fell straight to the grave. Many of the Jews when they saw it, started to rebel. They jumped on the Germans and escaped. The single ones. The older couldn't throw away the children. Over 1,000 in one day [were killed]. Fifty escaped. I was 18.

"I still believe in the existence of God. I still believe it, I still pray to God, and my children pray. But still I can't get over the fact that God permitted such a crime. I can't find an answer. I was trying to read and study, and even our religious authorities try to avoid this question. The idea of His existence, that's not questioned, but His action at this movement, in the Holocaust, that is questionable. It was an unmerciful God on this morning.

"We have no other substitute to depend on, to pray to. Sometimes I'm bitter at God."

"IF WE GIVE UP GOD, THAT'S IT"

Lea Spiro, a gift shop owner from Los Angeles, was from Radom, Poland. She was in five concentration camps from 1940 to 1945.

"I was only 14 when the whole thing started. Our house was traditional Jewish. You observe the Holy Days. You keep kosher. I never thought about it before it happened, I was taught that there was a God, and I believed it. Now I am married to an Orthodox Jew. I do believe in God, of course. I think I have the same belief. Of course you blame God. You just blame. You blame.

"If everyone would deny God, there wouldn't be any reason for being Jewish any more. It's a way of life. Everything is just in a frame of believing in God.

"There are so few of us left now, if we give up God, that's it. Hitler has won. What he

couldn't do in the concentration camps, we would do ourselves.

"I had a very close friend, a boy that I went to school with. He was born in a courtyard [apartment building built around a courtyard] and grew up with a boy and they were always playing together. It was in 1940 when they took us into the ghetto. Anyone who told where a Jew was hiding would get one kilo of sugar — that's two pounds. And that friend of his knew where he was hiding, so he brought the Germans there and they shot him.

"In Poland, when you were born in one of those courtyards, you lived there all your life. All the kids played outside, were together always. This was just one example, but there were so many. They used to come and look into the ghetto and laugh and laugh their heads off. When the Germans came to Poland, they couldn't tell who was a Jew and who wasn't a Jew. I was blond and blue-eyed. The first German word the Poles learned was Jude. If the Gentiles hadn't helped, he couldn't have done the job.

"The Poles were all Christians, Catholics, there. The Poles were a very depressed country, and the priests said this is the reason you are economically depressed. They were telling them the Jews killed Jesus. [Before the war] we had a [housekeeper]. She was a country girl. She asked my mother, why did you have to do that, why did you kill Jesus.

"The Germans didn't do it because of religion, but the Poles did.

"My mother was planting something. They laughed and said, a Jew can't grow anything. You see, for hundreds of years [occupations were restricted]. A Jew can be a moneylender, a merchant; he cannot be a teacher, a bureaucrat; he cannot own land.

"In a work camp, we [planned] to escape. I was the eighth one. I caught my thigh in the barbed wire and went back. They [the other seven] were shot by the Polish underground. I would have been dead, too. There were two Polish undergrounds. One was the Polish communist, and they accepted Jews. And then there was the national underground; when they caught a Jew in the forest, they shot him."

(Top) Five Jews are lined up against a wall shortly before being shot by German soldiers.
(Above) These women partisan fighters, in ragged clothes that they scrounged and pearls from more elegant times, fought the Germans with makeshift weapons before being captured.
(Left below) A roundup of Jews in the Warsaw Ghetto.
(Left above) When the British liberated Bergen-Belsen, they found more than 10,000 bodies in the camp, many dead from starvation or disease.
Trenches were dug, and the former prison guards and German civilians buried the dead.

THEOLOGIANS PONDER HOLOCAUST'S CAUSES

BY PAULA HERBUT

Lea Spiro, a Holocaust survivor now living in Los Angeles, still remembers the taunts of Christian children when she was growing up in the 1930s in Radom, Poland.

"You could play with the kids in the courtyard, and all of a sudden they would say, 'Hey, you're a Jew, you killed Jesus,'" she said. From the taunts of children to the forced wearing of a Star of David to five concentration camps, she told of the tightening net of isolation with the onslaught of Nazi Germany.

The taunts of children came from erroneous theology. But, according to theologians examining the Holocaust, such theology was taught for centuries in churches around the world, leading to pogroms, to persecution, and finally to the climate permitting Hitler's plan to kill the worldwide Jewish population.

Spiro was one of more than 10,000 survivors who came to the American Gathering of Jewish Holocaust Survivors in Washington. Six million Jews — one-third the world's Jewish population — perished in the Holocaust.

For Jews, the establishment and support of the State of Israel is one outcome of the Holocaust. Another is reexamination of Jewish theology and Jewish identity. Christians, meanwhile, are sorting through centuries of church-promoted anti-Semitism, trying to eliminate anti-Semitic teachings, and revising concepts of Christianity in relation to Judaism.

The Rev. Dr. Franklin Littell, founder of the Philadelphia-based National Institute on the Holocaust and a professor of religion at Temple University in Philadelphia, said the Holocaust leads to a "credibility crisis" for both the modern university, which produced "technically competent barbarians," and Christianity. "This monstrous crime was committed by baptized Catholics, Protestants, and Orthodox Christians, none of them rebuked, let alone excommunicated."

"One cannot escape the implications of the Christian responsibility, because Christians have taught for centuries, and preached, contempt for the Jewish people," said Littell, a United Methodist minister.

"The question also arises, why didn't Christians help the Jews more than they did? How did a terrorist movement like the German Nazi power come to power with the kind of ideology it was proclaiming without church leaders digging in and preaching against it ever coming to power?

"It was all there in perfectly clear writing in the party platform and in Hitler's *Mein Kampf*. Some were afraid that the communists were going to take over Europe. Some were such fanatical patriots they would have supported the devil himself if he were German, and he was. And a good many of them were just naturally compromisers and accommodators, bureaucrats."

The Rev. Dr. John T. Pawlikowski, a Roman Catholic priest and professor of social ethics at the Catholic Theological Union in Chicago, said that "traditional, primarily Christian anti-Semitism served as an indispensable seed bed for the popular acceptance of the Nazi genocidal plan."

Faulty theology included the charge that Jews killed Jesus and the perpetual wandering concept, which said Jews were to roam the world without a state of their own as a sign of punishment for not accepting Jesus as the Messiah, he said. There also were the fables: in the Catholic Church, there was the "blood libel charge" from the Middle Ages, that Jews killed Christian children and drank the blood during a seder. There are probably some who "still believe it," Pawlikowski said.

Lay Catholic Holocaust scholar Harry Cargas, professor of literature and language at Webster University at St. Louis and author of *A Christian Response to the Holocaust*, called the Holocaust "the greatest Christian tragedy since the crucifixion . . ."

"In history," he said, "we had ghettoization of Jews, expulsion from nations, the Inquisition . . . Then it turned from theological anti-Semitism to racial anti-Semitism. That started in the 19th century.

"Hitler didn't just happen on the scene. He did what he did only because it was possible to do. In the middle 1930s, Hitler embarked on a 'euthanasia' campaign, killing the feeble, mentally unproductive, the aged. He killed about 50,000 people. The Christian churches spoke out, and Hitler abandoned the euthanasia program. What would have happened if there had been a [Papal] encyclical for the Jews? There's reason to believe it would have saved millions of lives."

Pope Pius XII was "silent," he charged.

"The annihilations went on, with impunity," Cargas said. Heinrich Himmler, "who insisted that members of the SS must believe in God, could thus, unchallenged by serious moral attacks, speak of the honor and decency of the work of slaughter: 'We can say that we have performed this task in love of our people. And we have suffered no damage from it in our inner self, in our soul, in our character,'" he said.

Among Cargas' suggestions are that the Catholic Church excommunicate Hitler, that the Christian liturgical calendars include an annual memorial service for Jewish victims of the Holocaust, that the Christian churches insist on the essential Jewishness of Christianity, and that the Christian emphasis on missionizing be "redirected toward perfecting individual Christian lives" instead.

Jews who tried to escape the Holocaust when it was still possible were turned away by many safe countries, including the United States.

The support of Israel as refuge is one result.

The Holocaust and the establishment of the State of Israel "mirror each other," said Rabbi Daniel Landes in the book of essays *Genocide: Critical Issues of the Holocaust.*

"As the Holocaust can be understood as Jewish powerlessness and victimization, Israel is the expression of Jewish power and self-determination," said Landes, director of research projects at the Simon Wiesenthal Center in Los Angeles.

"We lost 80 percent of all the rabbis, scholars, artists, poets, historians," said Rabbi Michael Berenbaum, a Holocaust scholar and executive director of the Jewish Community Council of Greater Washington. "The Jewish people learned the perils of powerlessness and homelessness, and that's the reason for our deep commitment to Israel.

The Holocaust raises "questions about God, with the simple question, where was God during the Holocaust; about the nature of man, and about the nature of the people of Israel," said Rabbi Seymour Siegel, executive director of the U.S. Holocaust Memorial Council.

One answer is that "evil in the world like the Holocaust is not created by God but is created by man," he said. "The evil of the Holocaust destroys all simple, optimistic views about human nature, and shows the depth of evil that persons can commit against other persons . . ."

The Holocaust differed from other genocidal examples because of its use of assembly-line technology in the slaughter. "It's a warning," said Holocaust survivor Rabbi Arthur Schneier, rabbi of Park East Synagogue in New York and chairman of the American division of the World Jewish Congress. For "haven't we perfected our technology?" he asked.

"Above all," he said, "the greatest danger is silence and indifference, whenever there is any kind of injustice. The one important lesson of the Holocaust is the slumber of indifference on the part of many good people who played it safe."

When the Allies entered the camps, they found thousands of corpses. Even after liberation, starved and sick prisoners continued to die. (Top) Members of a British Parliamentary delegation visit Buchenwald. Bodies of men who died during the preceding 24 hours are stacked, awaiting burial. (Above) The U.S. First Army found these skeletonlike bodies when they entered the camp at Nordhausen, Germany, where slave laborers of various nationalities, some dead and some dying, lay side by side. (Left) Bodies of gassed prisoners were disposed of in adjoining crematoria, where other prisoners were forced to burn the dead.

A PERMANENT MEMORIAL TO SIX MILLION SLAIN

BY PHIL McCOMBS

> **"** At 12 o'clock noon one day we lined up to get hot water to warm up. It was our soup. We lined up to the cans of soup. This German copa [term for German camp guard, often a common criminal], this short fella, he maybe a gangster or something in Germany, he takes these cans of soup and starts spilling them. He says being that we didn't work, we didn't deserve it. I had my pick in my hands and I jump out of line. I grab him and before I was going to hit him I said, "German officers have the right to do this. You don't have right." The German commandant rode up on his horse then. He slapped me in the face with his gloves. He said, "You got saved by saying a German officer can do it." **"**

Joseph Gordon, 57, Silver Spring businessman. Born in Lithuania. Imprisoned in Auschwitz and Muldorf.

The U.S. government confirmed March 3, 1983 that it has allocated two large, vacant brick buildings 400 yards southeast of the Washington Monument and adjacent to the national Mall for a $30- to $40-million Holocaust museum.

The decision to place the memorial museum — in memory of Jewish and other Holocaust victims — so prominently, plus its large scale and the official status conferred by its congressional mandate, represent an extraordinary American commitment to remember one of history's darkest periods. The only other memorial on this scale is Israel's Yad Vashem in Jerusalem.

"My hope is that whoever will enter this museum will leave it a different person," said Elie Wiesel, chairman of the U.S. Holocaust Memorial Council, an independent federal agency set up by Congress in 1980 to raise private funds to create the memorial museum.

"Our hope is to create a living museum, not stones, but experiences, memorials, ideas, to keep the past alive . . . for the sake of future generations." Completion is scheduled for mid-1987.

Wiesel, a survivor of Auschwitz and Buchenwald and now a Boston University professor, said transfer of the buildings to the Holocaust council will be announced officially — perhaps by President Reagan — during the Days of Remembrance of the Holocaust, April 10 through 17. Nearly 20,000 concentration camp survivors are expected to meet then in Washington.

Wiesel said the council will announce a $75-million national fund drive for construction and the museum's programs. The council has an $820,000 federally funded budget this year and has asked for $1,953,000 next year. But Wiesel said he hoped in the future "we don't need the taxpayers' money."

The 138-percent budget increase for next year is needed to pay the sharply increasing number of design, engineering, audio-visual, computer and other consultants required to plan the museum, according to Micah H. Naftalin, the council's senior deputy director. "We've now gone critical with the planning," he said. "It's a major undertaking."

Council officials are negotiating to get a third, smaller building adjacent to the two they have, a General Services Administration spokesman said yesterday.

Council Vice Chairman Mark Talisman said building the memorial museum is "a hell of a challenge. It's going to take every American to get involved . . . It will be an enormous place of learning, of caring . . . It's a museum and memorial to six million Jews and millions of others who died . . . Does one call it a Jewish memorial? No, not by any means. The dimensions will be much broader than that."

Among those designated for persecution and death by the Nazis were Gypsies, slavs, Jehovah's Witnesses, homosexuals, political opponents and others. Talisman added that the Holocaust and any related memorial must always have a special meaning for Jews — an entire race targeted for extinction by the Nazis.

Naftalin said, "It's by no means an ethnic or Jewish museum. It's for the whole American people. There will be an emphasis on the role of the liberators" and exhibits noting groups other than Jews who died in the camps.

The Sept. 29, 1979, report by the Commission on the Holocaust appointed by President Carter — which recommended building a memorial museum in Washington — said "special emphasis would also be placed on the American aspect of the Holocaust — the absence of American response (exclusion of refugees, denials of the Holocaust), the American liberation of the camps, the reception of the survivors after 1945, the lives rebuilt in this country and their contribution to American society . . ."

Wiesel chaired the commission as well as the council that Congress and the Reagan administration later created to implement commission recommendations.

Planning for the memorial museum is still in its early stages, but officials say it will include exhibits to evoke the horror of the Holocaust, an education program aimed at youth, scholarly programs linked with universities around the world and possibly an advanced computer setup to store documents and the names of Holocaust victims.

Extensive consideration is being given by the 65-member council — which includes Jewish leaders, members of Congress and others — to such delicate questions as how children can be exposed to the terrible material in the museum without being traumatized — or even if this is possible.

The two buildings were transferred by the GSA to the council through the Interior Department, the council's parent agency, according to a GSA spokesman. Both Interior Secretary James Watt and GSA Administrator Gerald P. Carmen attended the council's last meeting in December at the Kennedy Center, where Carmen was given an award by the council for his help.

"From evil and from disaster and from all those type of things, good things do come," Carmen responded, according to a transcript. "And if I can just be a non-government official and just be a Jew for a moment, I think that those years that we were growing up in America [during the Holocaust] and that trauma that we all went through did a lot for us [to help us] very personally know how much democracy means and how much freedom means." He said the memorial will "be held as a symbol of what can happen when [we] let down our guard."

According to the same transcript, Watt said the memorial "must be much more than a tribute to the dead. It must be a reminder to the living of the horrors which can be inflicted when tyrannical powers are allowed to gain the military, economic and strategic advantage to do as they will without fear of retribution."

The two buildings are known as Annex One and Two of the old auditor's complex stretching from 14th to 15th Street along Independence Avenue NW. Council officials said engineering studies of the buildings' structural soundness are under way, but it will be another year before an architect is chosen.

The turn-of-the-century buildings, with 32,000 square feet of space, are long, rambling, two-story red brick structures with a varied history. When they were built, they served as stables and laundry buildings. At one time or another they were used by the Agriculture Department, the Bureau of Engraving and Printing, Bureau of Hatcheries and other agencies. Many of the windows are broken and much of the inside space is dusty and dirty. But from the 15th Street side of the complex there are sweeping views of the Jefferson Memorial, the Tidal Basin and the Washington Monument.

Distinguishing features are the picturesque roof line, towers, small cupolas and clerestory.

Rep. Sidney Yates (D-Ill.), a council member who helped push the memorial legislation through Congress, recalled how affected the council members were by the buildings when they first saw them. "It reminded some of the members who had just returned from the death camps in Europe of the shape of the buildings in Auschwitz," Yates said. "It had that same overall general shape."

The council's museum-planning team is headed by Rabbi Seymour Siegel of the Jewish Theological Seminary, and includes Anna Cohn, past director of the B'nai B'rith museum here; Jesaja Weinberg, director of the Museum of the Diaspora in Tel Aviv; Harvard professor Erich Goldhagen, a Holocaust survivor, and Sister Mary Glynn of the Bishop Kearney High School in Brooklyn.

So far the council has not decided whether to commission a separate work of sculpture or other art, according to Naftalin.

THE MEMORIAL: A CLASSIC POLITICAL SUCCESS STORY

BY PHIL McCOMBS

On a spring afternoon two years ago, members of the U.S. Holocaust Memorial Council visited two surplus federal buildings near the Washington Monument. The council was considering sites for America's official Museum of the Holocaust.

The long, two-story red brick buildings were ideally located, between 14th and 15th streets NW near the Mall, but were crumbling and filthy, with broken windows and junk-filled rooms. They had a barracks-like appearance: "I'll never forget if I live to be a thousand," said Council member Hyman Bookbinder. "When I approached the buildings I looked at them and I said, 'Oh my God, this looks like Auschwitz.'"

The members gathered in a big room in one building. Silence fell. "It was very eerie and wonderful and everybody was feeling the same," said vice chairman Mark Talisman. "I was in tears . . . Others cried . . ."

Chairman Elie Wiesel, a survivor of Auschwitz and Buchenwald, said quietly in his Hungarian accent, "This is it. This is it."

The Holocaust museum project was born in partisan politics in the Carter White House, and its history includes bitter squabbling over political appointments. But, in many ways, it is a classic political success story. Two presidents and a unanimous Congress endorsed it, and officials as diverse as Stuart Eizenstat and James G. Watt labored so that an edifice bearing testament to the darkest in human nature will overlook the Mall, America's spacious, upbeat hymn to the Enlightenment.

Keys to the $6.1 million building were handed to Wiesel by Vice President Bush as part of the Days of Remembrance of Victims of the Holocaust. Planning is going forward with $2.4 million in federal money, and the council is seeking $75 million in private funds to create the museum and a related educational, archival and research foundation. Officials hope to open the doors by late 1988.

The idea was always to keep the project above politics. "Partisanship could kill it instantly," said Talisman. Wiesel objected when a public relations person was hired because, he said, "It's too holy for that."

The subject — the effort to exterminate an entire people — is at once so horrifying, personal and universal that its entry into the homogenizing maw of American politics was, for many, unthinkable.

Yet others believe the museum is a necessity. The survivors of the death camps are dying, the documentation moldering. An institute in California has claimed the Holocaust never happened. Making it part of the larger American consciousness risks dilution and distortion, wrote former project official Michael Berenbaum, but "if we choose not to run these risks, we cannot bemoan the fact that the world is ignorant or indifferent."

The history of the project includes unusual measures to hide developments from the public, infighting over which groups to include and angry debate on the definition of the Holocaust itself. Turkey has warned that including the 1915-1923 Armenian genocide as a precursor to the Holocaust will strain relations, and the German ambassador has privately expressed concern.

But the museum is unstoppable now.

"I saw the Mall surrounded by monuments and museums testifying to the greatness of our civilization," said Council member and Auschwitz survivor Sigmund Strochlitz. ". . . And here [will] be a memorial to a failure. Auschwitz perverted the values of Western civilization, and all of a sudden in the heart of Washington we are going to have a monument to that perversion. It's amazing."

The museum had its origin at a time of bitter U.S.-Israeli relations when American Jews feared a Carter administration tilt to the Arabs. The initial spark was moral as well as political.

On March 27, 1978, Ellen Goldstein of the Carter domestic policy staff read a column by William Safire on American neo-Nazi plans to march in Skokie, Illinois. "America has no vivid reminder of the horror of the Final Solution," wrote Safire.

In 1977, Goldstein had been asked by Mark A. Siegel, Carter's liaison with American Jewish voters, to research Holocaust memorials in other countries. Now, as she read of the neo-Nazis, she remembered the memorial project, and on March 28 sent a memo to domestic policy chief Stuart Eizenstat suggesting the administration promote a memorial even though this "might appear . . . to be glib public relations."

A week earlier, Carter and Israeli Prime Minister Menachem Begin had finished two days of talks in sharp disagreement. Earlier in the month the Israelis had invaded Lebanon over U.S. protests. Carter's plan to sell warplanes to Egypt and Saudi Arabia had outraged American Jews, and Mark Siegel had resigned from the White House March 8 in protest.

"I was really intrigued with [the Goldstein memo]," said Eizenstat, "in part because I myself lost a number of relatives in the Holocaust. I thought it was terribly important that documentation be made so clear that no one could ever seriously question" the reality and scope of the Holocaust.

While the Goldstein memo was on Eizenstat's desk, NBC's mini-series *Holocaust* mesmerized Americans in mid-April. On April 25 Eizenstat sent a memo to Carter noting "stronger support than ever among many Americans — not just Jewish-Americans — for an official U.S. memorial . . . to the Holocaust victims."

He suggested Carter announce plans for a

"I'll never forget it if I live to be a thousand," one Holocaust Memorial Council member recalled of his first visit to the building designated to be the Holocaust Memorial Museum in Washington (exterior, top and interior above). "When I approached the buildings I looked at them and I said, 'Oh my God, this looks like Auschwitz.'"
(Left) The keys to the museum were formally turned over to Council chairman Elie Wiesel (left) by Vice President George Bush (right) at a ceremony in front of the Capitol on April 13, 1983.

memorial at a May 1, 1978 White House ceremony honoring Israel's 30th anniversary. Begin, hundreds of rabbis and other guests would be there. Carter agreed. In his speech, Carter asserted "our absolute commitment to Israel's security." The memorial would be "to the six million who were killed in the Holocaust."

Begin called the speech "one of the greatest moral statements ever."

The skies seemed to be clearing; the Camp David accords lay just five months ahead.

Carter and Eizenstat agreed there was only one person of sufficient stature to chair the commission, and Eizenstat phoned Elie Wiesel.

An author and scholar, Wiesel is best known for his writings on the death camps, where he lost his parents and younger sister. After meeting alone with Carter in the Oval Office, he accepted the job.

Wiesel "wanted to be sure it would be depoliticized," said Eizenstat. "I assured him it would be bipartisan."

Eizenstat and Carter chose Irving Greenberg of the National Jewish Resource Center as commission director, and Berenbaum, a religion professor at Wesleyan, as deputy. Eizenstat also phoned Sen. Jacob Javits (R-N.Y.) and Rep. Sidney Yates (D-Ill.), deans of the Jewish delegations in Congress.

Full exterior view of the buildings (outlined) to be the Holocaust Memorial Museum on the Mall.

Yates later became central to the project by spearheading the drive to get congressional approval.

The commission was launched Nov. 1, 1978, with 24 members and 27 advisers. They included a range of Jewish and Christian scholars and leaders. One member, Sen. John C. Danforth (R-Mo.), is an Episcopal minister who was so moved by the *Holocaust* mini-series that in 1979 he persuaded Congress to make April 28 and 29 the first nationwide Days of Remembrance.

From the first, said Berenbaum, "There was a debate . . . as to the nature of who are the victims, what is the unique Jewish dimension.

There was also the question of whether it should be in New York or Washington. Were we talking about a national memorial or a Jewish memorial built under national auspices?"

Wiesel knew what he wanted — a memorial museum on the scale of Israel's Holocaust center, Yad Vashem in Jerusalem, a center of learning, a shrine. "I managed to turn it around," he said. "They meant to have a monument costing $100,000. I began saying, 'No.' It's possible to influence people, to change things.

"It began as a political thing, but it became much more."

announcement never took place, nor did the council's federally paid public relations person ever announce the transfer, which was made public in a newspaper account in March, 1983.

That April 24, a Holocaust commemoration ceremony was held in the Rotunda by Carter and congressional leaders. Eizenstat called it

representative to the United Nations War Crimes Commission.

No sooner was the museum's prominent

Operations Division (general staff) "balked" at bombing because it did not want such an extra burden while fighting a war.

A prime case in point involves a claim made repeatedly by the War Department: Birkenau could be attacked by B17 and B24 heavy bombers only from distant British bases. McCloy himself last made that claim on Nov. 18, 1944, in rejecting a strong appeal by John W. Pehle, executive director of the War Refugee Board, to bomb the gas chambers and crematoria.

Repeating a passage in a draft memo from the Operations Division for Assistant Chief of Staff J.E. Hull, McCloy said: "Use of heavy bombardment from United Kingdom bases would necessitate a round trip flight unescorted of approximately 2,000 miles over enemy territory." His memo also reflected Hull's view that "the proposal is of very doubtful feasibility and is unacceptable from a military standpoint at this time in that it would be a diversion from our strategic bombing effort and the results obtained would not justify the high losses likely to result from such a mission."

Today, similarly, McCloy says that Gen. Arnold had opposed such "deep penetration" strikes, saying they would entail sending 35 to 50 B17 or B24 heavy bombers on special missions too long to allow fighter escorts throughout, bring "very heavy casualties" to U.S. airmen, kill inmates while inciting Nazi "reprisals" against them, and still be ineffective.

But neither in 1944 nor in 1983 did McCloy (or Hull) hint at — if they knew — a revealing fact that became widely known in 1978: For six months, the U.S. 15th Air Force, based not in England but at Foggia in southern Italy, had been regularly demonstrating the feasibility of air strikes on Birkenau. The 15th was doing this with its all-out effort to destroy the cluster of at least eight Nazi synthetic fuel plants in Poland near Upper Silesian coal mines. Buna was one of them.

McCloy told me he was unaware of the 15th's effort but added that at the time, he "must have known" or "probably heard of" it. This would seem to confirm Wyman's belief, set out in a May 1978 Commentary article, that "the possibilities were never investigated in Washington."

The 15th reached its full authorized strength by May 1944, weeks after the Luftwaffe had become a defeated force. On May 8, Wyman wrote, Lt. Gen. Ira C. Eaker, chief of Allied air forces in Italy, assured Air Force leaders that his heavy bombers could make daylight raids on Blechhammer, an oil plant 47 miles from Auschwitz, and that others at Auschwitz and Odertal "might also be attacked simultaneously."

In late June, the 15th began to bomb Buna and other plants as few as 13 miles from Auschwitz. In all, the 15th's B17s and B24s flew more than 2,280 sorties to attack targets close to Birkenau, dropping up to 10 times that many bombs. Contrary to the claims Hull and McCloy were making in November, P51 Mustangs and late-model P38 fighters had been escorting the heavy bombers regularly since May.

The Foggia bases not only didn't require overflights of Germany but, as the crow flies, they were about 25 percent closer than Britain was to the cluster of German oil plants. Buna, 750 miles from London, was only 600 miles from Foggia. Where the "2,000-mile, round-

trip" figure originated, McCloy says, he doesn't know.

Years later, Birkenau was noticed to be "in perfect alignment" with Buna by Dino A. Brugioni, a retired CIA senior official and expert on aerial reconnaissance and photo interpretation. Brugioni says an aircraft flying to or returning from Buna had to fly directly over the death factory. McCloy says that "I didn't know" either of the alignment or of the closeness of Birkenau to Buna.

In four raids on Buna between Aug. 20 and Dec. 26, 1944, the 15th dropped 3,394 high-explosive, 500-pound bombs. The first attack was by 127 B17s strongly protected by 100 Mustangs. Antiaircraft guns protecting Buna and Birkenau and 19 defending German fighter planes "were ineffective," Wyman wrote. "Only one American bomber went down; no Mustangs were hit." The second strike, by 96 B24 Liberators Sept. 13, met no Nazi fighters, but heavy flak from guns emplaced during the preceding three weeks shot down three bombers.

At this stage, destruction of the death installations would have all but guaranteed that they would not be rebuilt, in Wyman's view, because the Nazis would have had "to commit new and virtually nonexistent manpower resources to mass killing." He said they preferred gas chambers because they were "far more efficient" than gunfire — they killed 2,000 people in less than half an hour and "required only a limited number of SS men. Killing tens of thousands by gunfire would have required a military force."

Starting April 4, 1944, photo reconnaisance planes based near Foggia flew more than 30 missions over Buna, always photographing Birkenau in the process. In a 1979 CIA monograph, Brugioni and Robert C. Poirier labeled "extermination operations in progress" on Aug. 25, 1944; they had dug out the Air Force photos of Birkenau in a year-long search on their own time.

If photo interpreters had been alerted, Brugioni says in the January-March issue of Military Intelligence, they "would have quickly located" the four gas chamber-crematoria buildings. McCloy says he had never inquired if there were aerial photos of Birkenau. There is no evidence to show that the 15th Air Force discovered or was told that Birkenau was a death factory.

McCloy says his involvement in the Auschwitz question began with a summons from Harry Hopkins, a top aide to FDR who died in 1946, to meet with him and possibly with the late Samuel Rosenman, regarded by some as the "special adviser to Roosevelt on Jewish affairs."

McCloy recalls Hopkins telling him that Jewish spokesmen had told FDR personally that they wanted bombings, but that "the Boss [Roosevelt] was not disposed to" bombing. Hopkins asked him "to inquire of the Air Force as to what the logistics were." McCloy said he already had Arnold's negative appraisal and gave it to Rosenman, and "that was the end of that."

But Wyman says: "I've been unable to find, in years of trying, any documentary evidence that the bombing question ever came to Roosevelt. FDR didn't care enough about the whole issue of rescue to let that issue or any aspect of it become a deep concern; would meet only once with Jewish groups to discuss it, and shunted their written appeals to the State Department."